SpringerBriefs in Psychology

Behavioral Criminology

Series Editor

Vincent B. Van Hasselt, Fort Lauderdale, FL, USA

Behavioral Criminology is a multidisciplinary approach that draws on behavioral research for the application of behavioral theories and methods to assessment, prevention, and intervention efforts directed toward violent crime and criminal behavior. Disciplines relevant to this field are criminology; criminal justice (law enforcement and corrections); forensic, correctional, and clinical psychology and psychiatry: neuropsychology, neurobiology, conflict and dispute resolution; sociology, and epidemiology. Areas of study and application include, but are not limited to: specific crimes and perpetrators (e.g., homicide and sex crimes, crimes against children, child exploitation, domestic, school, and workplace violence), topics of current national and international interest and concern (e.g., terrorism and counter terrorism, cyber crime), and strategies geared toward evaluation, identification, and interdiction with regard to criminal acts (e.g., hostage negotiation, criminal investigative analysis, threat and risk assessment). The aim of the proposed Briefs is to provide practitioners and researchers with information, data, and current best practices on important and timely topics in Behavioral Criminology. Each Brief will include a review of relevant research in the area, original data, implications of findings, case illustrations (where relevant), and recommendations for directions that future efforts might take.

More information about this series at http://www.springer.com/series/10850

Christine M. Sarteschi

Sovereign Citizens

A Psychological and Criminological Analysis

Christine M. Sarteschi
Chatham University
Pittsburgh, PA, USA

ISSN 2192-8363　　　　　　　ISSN 2192-8371　(electronic)
SpringerBriefs in Psychology
ISSN 2194-1866　　　　　　　ISSN 2194-1874　(electronic)
SpringerBriefs in Behavioral Criminology
ISBN 978-3-030-45850-8　　　ISBN 978-3-030-45851-5　(eBook)
https://doi.org/10.1007/978-3-030-45851-5

© The Author(s), under exclusive license to Springer Nature Switzerland AG 2020, Corrected Publication 2020
All rights are reserved by the Publisher, whether the whole or part of the material is concerned, specifically the rights of translation, reprinting, reuse of illustrations, recitation, broadcasting, reproduction on microfilms or in any other physical way, and transmission or information storage and retrieval, electronic adaptation, computer software, or by similar or dissimilar methodology now known or hereafter developed.
The use of general descriptive names, registered names, trademarks, service marks, etc. in this publication does not imply, even in the absence of a specific statement, that such names are exempt from the relevant protective laws and regulations and therefore free for general use.
The publisher, the authors, and the editors are safe to assume that the advice and information in this book are believed to be true and accurate at the date of publication. Neither the publisher nor the authors or the editors give a warranty, expressed or implied, with respect to the material contained herein or for any errors or omissions that may have been made. The publisher remains neutral with regard to jurisdictional claims in published maps and institutional affiliations.

This Springer imprint is published by the registered company Springer Nature Switzerland AG
The registered company address is: Gewerbestrasse 11, 6330 Cham, Switzerland

Introduction

Jesse James and Billy the Kid are two unabashed criminals from our American past. They lived outside the law and were thus labeled "outlaws." They could have conducted their criminal activity under other labels, for instance "sovereign citizen," but their activities were still outside the law and as such could be most simply and best labeled as "outlaws."

The behavior of sovereign citizens, in every case, is also outside the law. They can best and most fittingly be labeled "outlaws." Sovereign citizens are not ignorant of the law. They know the law as well as every other American citizen. They simply choose to live outside the law, because it benefits them. Their lives are enriched by not following the law. They do not register their vehicles, they do not acquire driver's licenses, they do not pay taxes, they lie to police, they refuse to identify themselves or identify themselves with false names, and at times they shoot and kill police officers. The Federal Bureau of Investigation (FBI) recognizes sovereign citizens as a serious domestic terrorist threat in the United States (U.S.). Though the FBI labels sovereign citizens as a terrorist threat they do not label them as a terrorist organization. Sovereign citizens are not a unified group but are a movement of loosely affiliated, similarly-minded, individuals.

Make no mistake about it, sovereign citizens with their selfish, criminal antics are a threat to the U.S. government and every law-abiding, non-sovereign citizen. The U.S. Constitution provides and mandates, the resolution of legal conflicts, opinions, etc., through a well-defined court system. The courts, the appellate courts and eventually the Supreme Court, will peacefully resolve legal conflicts. Opposing parties may not agree on the courts opinions but they will abide by the court's decisions. The validity of a law, its application and its meaning, is determined by the American judicial system. The final word lies within the province of the American judicial system. To deny the jurisdiction of the American court system over every person, American, non-American, citizen, noncitizen, living within the borders of the U.S. is a statement of anarchy. It is a threat to the U.S. government and thus the reason why the FBI recognizes sovereign citizens as being a serious domestic terrorist threat. Sovereign citizens, through their actions, live outside the law and thus also must be thought of as "outlaws."

This book is about the dangers of sovereign citizens, their history and methods to effectively deal with the threat they pose. Broadly speaking, sovereign citizens are considered an antigovernment "patriot" group whose core beliefs sometimes overlap with other far-right extremist groups. They are capable of committing violent crimes including mass murder, rape, kidnapping, bank robbery, and many others. They flood the courts with frivolous pseudolegal claims via a well-known tactic called paper terrorism. They reject the validity of the American legal system. They reject the validity of the American government itself. Relative to other antigovernmental groups in society, sovereign citizens have received very little scholarly attention. That is surprising given the threat that they pose to law enforcement. In his 2016 congressional testimony concerning terrorism, Orange County, Florida Sheriff Jerry Demings stated that "…sovereign citizens pose one of the most significant threats to civilian law enforcement today" (Stopping the Next Attack: How to Keep Our City Streets from Becoming the Battleground 2016). He is not alone in his views. A 2013 survey of law-enforcement intelligence officers, rated sovereign citizens as being the biggest domestic terrorist threat (up from seventh in the 2006 survey). They felt this terrorist threat to be greater than even the threat of homegrown Islamic terrorists (Carter et al. 2014). Nevada's attorney general recently testified that sovereign citizens represent the largest terrorism threat facing the state (Solis 2019).

This book argues that sovereign citizens are especially dangerous and deserving of greater attention. For the purpose of this book, sovereign citizens (as they are referred to in the U.S.) are a subculture of individuals who believe that the American government is illegitimate and holds no authority over anyone who recognizes themselves as being "sovereign." They vehemently reject being citizens of the U.S. Their logic is that since the U.S. government is illegitimate, law enforcement officers, the judicial system and all other governmental representatives, have no authority over them. Sovereign citizens have no respect for the existing laws of America.

They consider themselves to be above the law. They have reinterpreted the Constitution such that existing law, the currently accepted law, is rejected and replaced, in their minds, by only laws that are favorable to themselves. They accomplish this by utilizing a mix of pseudolegal and conspiracy-laden arguments. The legal merits of their arguments have been rejected by every judge in every court room in which they have appeared. In the quest to defend what they consider their rights as sovereigns, many have committed criminal acts, some of which have involved extreme violence. Often their anger is aimed at public officials, government facilities, financial institutions, the Internal Revenue Service (IRS) and the U.S. Treasury for the purpose of furthering their claim of immunity from government authority (U.S. Department of Homeland Security 2014; FBI 2017). No one knows with accuracy how many sovereigns there are in the U.S. but estimates range from 300,000 to 500,000 with expectations of continued growth (Southern Poverty Law Center n.d.)

There is no official definition of a sovereign citizen. Anyone can self-identify as a sovereign citizen by simply making the claim. There is no formal sovereign citizen organization. There is no sovereign citizen "membership" card. They are leaderless, loosely organized at best, and can be likened to anarchists. Because of this, a high degree of variability exists among adherents. This variability might be best exemplified by an FBI special agent tasked with investigating sovereign citizens in Montana: "It's a bit like Forrest Gump with the box of chocolates. You never know what you're going to get" (Bermes 2018 para. 4).

Different government agencies have varying definitions of what constitutes a sovereign citizen. The FBI provides the following definition. Sovereign citizens are "individuals who openly reject their U.S. citizenship status, believe that most forms of established government, authority, and institutions are illegitimate, and seek, wholly or in part, through unlawful acts of force or violence, to further their claim to be immune from government authority. The mere advocacy of political or social positions, political activism, use of strong rhetoric, or generalized philosophic embrace of violent tactics may not constitute extremism and may be constitutionally protected" (FBI 2017 p. 2). The difference that they are suggesting is that the philosophical advocacy of violence is not the same as actually committing violence.

Similarly, the Department of Homeland Security (DHS) also has a definition. They refer to them as sovereign citizen *extremists* which is defined as: "groups or individuals who facilitate or engage in acts of violence directed at public officials, financial institutions, and government facilities in support of their belief that the legitimacy of the U.S. citizenship should be rejected; almost all forms of established government, authority, and institutions are illegitimate; and that they are immune from federal, state and local laws" (U.S. Department of Homeland Security 2014 p. 1). The addition of the word "extremists" would seem to suggest that they are making a distinction between sovereign citizens who do not engage in violence and those that do engage in violence.

A wealth of information about sovereign citizens can be found on YouTube. They routinely record and upload videos of themselves interacting with public officials attempting to argue their way out of law violations. The videos of traffic stops, from police camera footage, are also readily available. Hundreds of thousands of videos are available and likely help to recruit new members. Their video recordings occur in public settings, often in court or in community buildings. Many of the recorded encounters involve traffic stops. Many sovereigns carry with them self-created, frivolous legal documents. Their "legal" documents are excerpted bits of law, strewn together by cherry-picking seemingly nonsensical (as one judge put it) "…centuries-old case law and obsolete legal dictionaries" insisting that it be read and that their interpretation of the law be upheld (United States v. Smith 2019). Some of the most popular video complications are of sovereigns getting "owned." These often feature sovereigns failing to effectively make their case to law enforcement and subsequently being tased, arrested, and in some cases, shot and killed. They repeatedly fail to convince authorities that their legal arguments have any validity, yet it does not dissuade other sovereigns from trying the same tactics and rhetoric.

Sovereign citizens are distinctly confrontational, antagonistic, argumentative, and litigious. They are characteristically bold and belligerent in their defense of their blatantly illegal behavior. They fervently argue their interpretation of the law, only to lose. They react with anger, shock and righteous indignation towards the police, when the officers are forced to break the windows of the sovereign citizen and forcefully withdraw them from their vehicles. Legal observers note that their actions are self-defeating and ill-advised. Yet, they continue their efforts, never dissuaded by their failures and the failures of sovereigns coming before them.

Given their unpredictable, often outlandish behavior and the use of ineffective tactics, it would be easy to presume that they are mentally ill. They have in fact been described as such. Many have characterized their behavior as bizarre, unusual, nonsensical, and delusional. In most cases, however, the sovereign citizen is not diagnosably mentally ill. There is no current diagnostic designation that fully captures the behavior of sovereign citizens. Certainly, there are cases involving sovereign citizens in which mental illness plays a role but they are the exception. When forced to undergo a court-ordered evaluation, almost all sovereign citizens are found to be without a diagnosable mental illness.

It is not that they struggle or fail to comprehend laws; competency testing by licensed clinicians finds that they are fully competent and have the capacity to make decisions. They refuse to accept conventional interpretations of the law and are choosing to operate outside the law. The majority of sovereign citizens understand their situation and are adept at articulating their beliefs. Put more simply, the claim of sovereign citizenship is a self-serving attempt to escape the law.

People who choose to break the law are by definition criminals. Prevention of crime is the goal of every society. The current measures that exist to combat sovereign citizens are not sufficient. New approaches are necessary to combat the immense problems sovereigns pose to our legal system and to all law-abiding citizens.

This book synthesizes the available information regarding sovereign citizens and puts forth new ideas for countering the sovereign citizen movement. The ideas presented here will hopefully serve as a foundation for future research and effective policy change.

References

Bermes, W. (2018, May 11). Law enforcement concerned about anti-government citizens. *Bozemandailychronicle.com*. Retrieved from https://www.bozemandailychronicle.com/news/crime/law-enforcement-concerned-about-anti-government-citizens/article_0fae9d46-d8bf-5629-8c25-8faf9b8a10c6.html?utm_medium=social&utm_source=twitter&utm_campaign=user-share

Carter, D., Chermak, S., Carter, J., & Drew, J. (2014). *Understanding law enforcement intelligence processes*. Report to the Office of University Programs, Science and Technology Directorate, U.S. Department of Homeland Security. College Park, MD: University of Maryland START Center.

Federal Bureau of Investigation. (2011). *Sovereign citizens: A growing domestic treat to law enforcement*. Washington, DC: Federal Bureau of Investigation, Counterterrorism Division. Retrieved from https://leb.fbi.gov/articles/featured-articles/sovereign-citizens-a-growing-domestic-threat-to-law-enforcement

Federal Bureau of Investigation. (2017). *Black identity extremists likely motivated to target law enforcement officers.* Washington, DC: Federal Bureau of Investigation, Counterterrorism Division.

Solis, J. (2019, August 21). White supremacism and 'changed face' of terrorism challenge Nevada authorities. *Nevada Current.* Retrieved from https://www.nevadacurrent.com/2019/08/21/white-supremacism-and-changed-face-of-terrorism-challenge-nevada-authorities/

Southern Poverty Law Center. (n.d.). *Sovereign citizens movement.* Retrieved from https://www.splcenter.org/fighting-hate/extremist-files/ideology/sovereign-citizens-movement

Stopping the Next Attack: How to Keep Our City Streets from Becoming the Battleground. Hearing Before Committee on Homeland Security, House of Representatives, 114th Cong. 44. (2016). (testimony of Sheriff Jerry L. Demings).

United States v. Smith. RDB-18-0271. *United states district court for the District of Maryland.* 2019. Retrieved from https://casetext.com/case/united-states-v-smith-362108

U.S. Department of Homeland Security. (2014). *Domestic violent extremists pose increased threat to government officials and law enforcement.* Washington, DC: Department of Homeland Security, Office of Intelligence and Analysis.

Contents

1 The Origins of the Sovereign Citizen Movement 1
   1.1 Tax Protestors 1
   1.2 Anti-Federalist 3
       1.2.1 The Posse Comitatus 3
   1.3 The Militia Movement 4
   1.4 Conclusion 6
   References 7

2 Behavior and Underlying Ideology 9
   2.1 Jurisdiction 10
   2.2 Warrants 11
   2.3 Joinder 11
   2.4 I Do Not Consent 12
   2.5 Traveling 12
   2.6 Refusing to Identify Themselves 13
   2.7 I Don't Answer Questions 13
   2.8 Self-Made License Plates 14
   2.9 Black's Law Dictionary 14
   2.10 What's the Emergency? 14
   2.11 Fee Schedules 15
   2.12 What's Your Bond Number? 15
   2.13 Do You Have a Business Card? 15
   2.14 Recording Traffic Stops or Live Broadcasting 16
   2.15 Calling 911 16
   2.16 Return Driver's License 17
   2.17 Revoking the Vehicle's Registration 18
   2.18 Not U.S. Citizens 19
   2.19 Driving Is a God-Given Right 19
   2.20 Not a Car, Truck or Vehicle 20
   2.21 Corpus Delicti 21
   2.22 Where Is the Injured Party? 23

	2.23	Did You Take an Oath?	24
	2.24	What Crime Am I Being Accused of Committing?	25
	2.25	Am I Being Detained?	26
	2.26	You Are Dismissed	27
	2.27	Lie to Police	27
	2.28	I Demand to Speak to Your Supervisor	28
3	**Violence and Sovereign Citizens**		31
	3.1	Andrew Joseph Stack	32
	3.2	Jerry Kane Jr. and Joseph Kane	32
	3.3	Nathaniel "Sach" Kargas	33
	3.4	Jered and Amanda Miller	34
	3.5	Stephen Paddock	34
	3.6	Travis Reinking	35
	3.7	Jared Loughner	35
	3.8	Terry Lyn Smith	36
	3.9	John Terry Chapman Jr	36
	3.10	Forrest Gordon Clark	36
	3.11	Scott Roeder	37
	3.12	Attempts, Threats, Unsuccessful Plots, and Jailhouse Conversions	38
	3.13	Janay Rebecca Smith	38
	3.14	Mitchell Timothy Taebel	39
	3.15	Michael Wayne Parsons	39
	3.16	Ted Klaudt	40
	3.17	Steven Lorenzo	41
	3.18	The Insane Deuces	42
	References		42
4	**Paper Terrorism and Other Tactics**		47
	4.1	What Is Paper Terrorism?	47
	4.2	False Liens	47
	4.3	OIDs and False Refund Cases	50
	4.4	"Bond Process"	50
	4.5	House Squatting	51
	4.6	Sovereign Citizen Fraud in U.S. Department of Housing and Urban Development (HUD) Programs	51
	4.7	Fraudulent Real Estate Ownership and Debt Elimination Services	52
	4.8	Midwives and Private Membership Associations (PMAs)	52
	4.9	Federal and State Laws Against Paper Terrorism	53
	4.10	Profile of A Paper Terrorist	54
	4.11	Conclusion	54
	References		55

5	Moors		59
	5.1	Origins of the Moors	60
	5.2	Moorish Sovereigns	61
	5.3	Moorish Sovereigns and Their Association With Other Groups	63
	5.4	The Nuwaubian Nation of Moors	63
	5.5	Islamic State in Iraq and Syria (ISIS)	65
	5.6	Scientology and the Anti-Vaccination Movement	65
	5.7	Violence Toward Law Enforcement By Moorish Sovereign Citizens	66
	References		68
6	Sovereign Citizens in Court		71
	6.1	Sovereign Citizens and Mental Illness	74
	6.2	Review of the Literature	74
	6.3	Female Sovereign Citizens	76
	References		80
7	Countering the Sovereign Citizen Movement		83
	7.1	Laws	83
	7.2	Squatting and Traffic Stops	84
	7.3	The Courts	86
	7.4	The Fight Against Domestic Terrorism	87
	References		89

Correction to: Sovereign Citizens: A Psychological and Criminological Analysis C1

The original version of this book was revised. The correction is available at
https://doi.org/10.1007/978-3-030-45851-5_8

About the Author

Christine M. Sarteschi LCSW is an Associate Professor of Social Work and Criminology. She teaches courses in behavioral science that cover a wide range of topics including: human behavior, juvenile justice, mental illness and crime, cold case research, problem solving courts, mass murder, and extreme violent crime. Her research has appeared in *The British Journal of Social Work*, *Aggression and Violent Behavior*, *The Journal of Criminal Justice*, among others. She has served as a peer reviewer for the National Science Foundation as well as other scholarly journals. Dr. Sarteschi's most recent Springer brief includes "Mass and Serial Murder in America."

Chapter 1
The Origins of the Sovereign Citizen Movement

Antigovernment sentiments have existed for many years. This chapter will discuss the short history and evolution of the antigovernment, sovereign citizen movement. It includes a discussion of groups, with similar ideas.

While there is no official history of the sovereign citizen movement, various other movements, beginning in the 1950s, have operated in similar ways using similar tactics. These include tax protestors, the Posse Comitatus, Christian identity adherents, patriot movement/militia (Loeser 2015; Berger 2016), and anti-Federalist groups (Perliger and Sweeney 2019). A common thread that exists amongst these aforementioned groups is their extreme dislike for government, their often-racist beliefs in the form of white supremacy, and their willingness to abuse the court system and to harass public officials (Loeser 2015). These groups will be discussed below.

1.1 Tax Protestors

The tax protest movement can be traced back to the 1950s. Much like modern day sovereign citizens, tax protesters were known to have used snippets of law and in some cases, biblical quotes, to justify their illegal behavior. One individual commonly associated with the movement is Arthur Porth, a building contractor from Wichita, Kansas (Berger 2016). Mr. Porth began filing court claims back in 1954, attempting to recover his income tax payments. Despite his many court room losses, Mr. Porth continued the fight against his paying income taxes. The judge who was associated with the case at the time, stated that Mr. Porth was "fanatical" in his belief in the unconstitutionality of the taxing and monetary system in the U.S. (Porth

---

The original version of this chapter was revised. The correction to this chapter is available at https://doi.org/10.1007/978-3-030-45851-5_8

v. the United States of America 1971). The court noted that his antipathy and fanaticism led to his 1967 conviction on tax evasion charges. He was sentenced to five years in prison (Levitas 2001).

Though Mr. Porth was largely unsuccessful in many of his efforts, he engaged in a number of tactics that are still attempted by sovereign citizens These include:

- Issuing illegal "arrest warrants" against officials who were allegedly violating the Constitution.
- Arguing that the 16th amendment (which authorized Congress to tax income) was unconstitutional because it was passed with the 15th amendment that freed slaves and as a result, only African Americans are expected to pay taxes (Semerad 1995). A later argument involving the 16th amendment suggested that it was never properly ratified because several states passed versions with variations in wording or punctuation (Baker 1986).
- The idea that paper money is not backed by gold or silver; taxpayers are not obligated to pay taxes because "Federal Reserve notes are not dollars" (Semerad 1995).
- Filing blank tax returns with the exception of a statement pleading the Fifth Amendment against self-incrimination ("Fifth Amendment Return") (Levitas 2001), a tactic common among far-right constitutionalists (Semerad 1995) utilized by others attempting to avoid paying their fair share.
- Arguing that wages gained from working are not taxable because they are an equal exchange for labor and thus no one makes a profit (Baker 1986).
- Attempting to utilize the "fringe-on-the-flag strategy" which suggested that they are free and sovereign individuals because they have no contract with the state (Baker 1986).

Other well-known tax protesters were eventually convicted and also sent to prison. This included Armen Condo, leader of the Garden Grove, California based Your Heritage Protection Association which, at its peak, claimed to have 27,000 members. The Internal Revenue Service (IRS) successfully prosecuted Condo on 41 counts of tax and mail fraud. He was sentenced to eight years in an Arizona prison and fined over $93,000. Personality-wise, Condo was described by those who knew him as being "the most glib person" (Baker 1986, p.1). Subsequently, the IRS was said to have brought nearly 600 Heritage Protection Association members to civil court and prosecuted another 30 on criminal charges.

Another victory for the government involved the prosecution of Dennis Riness of Tustin-based TEA, an Association of Twentieth-Century Patriots (Baker 1986). This Orange County, California group was said to have had between 3000 and 4000 members at its peak. After pleading guilty to aiding and assisting in the preparation of false income tax returns, Riness was sentenced to 13 months in prison, ordered to pay a $5000 fine and mandated to engage in community service. Riness had also been involved in tax shelter schemes involving a church. Eventually, the IRS succeeded in revoking its tax-exempt status. Soon thereafter, the association was effectively curtailed.

The aforementioned IRS victories, which helped lead to a significant reduction in the number of tax protesters, stemmed not only from prosecuting the offenders but enacting harsher penalties, including jail time and significant fines (Baker 1986). New laws made it more difficult for individuals to get away with not paying their taxes. Since then, laws surrounding tax penalties have continued to become more stringent. In 2008, for instance, the actor Wesley Snipes was sentenced to three years in federal prison for willfully failing to file his tax returns (*The New York Times*, 2008). According to *The New York Times*, Mr. Snipes was a member of American Rights Litigators, an organization that is alleged to have engaged in tax evasion schemes (2008). The organization was run by one of Mr. Snipes's codefendants, Mr. Kahn. During his trial, Mr. Kahn represented himself and refused to recognize the judge's authority, two common courtroom tactics used by sovereign citizens. Mr. Kahn was ultimately convicted and sentenced to 10 years in federal prison.

1.2 Anti-Federalist

Researchers categorize sovereign citizens as belonging to multiple movements including antigovernment, the far-right, and also anti-Federalist (Perliger and Sweeney 2019). The anti-Federalist movement emerged in the 1970s and its main goal was to undermine the federal government. Perliger and Sweeney (2019) explain that the movement was guided by three main ideas: (1) that the government is seeking to strip Americans from their rights; (2) a shadow government, controlled by the United Nations, would be a part of the "New World Order" and would be the result of a left-wing globalist conspiracy (Pitcavage 2001); (3) high-ranking Jewish conspirators are attempting to overtake the U.S. government. In their conspiracy-oriented belief systems, they also fear that the U.S. has already been corrupted by foreign actors (Perliger and Sweeney 2019). Many of these same ideas underlie the thinking of sovereign citizens.

1.2.1 The Posse Comitatus

Some researchers contend that the sovereign citizen movement has its roots in the Posse Comitatus (Valeri and Borgeson 2018; Loeser 2015). Posse Comitatus is a Latin term that means "power of the county" (Toy n.d.). It is the legal power granted to sheriffs and other county officials to summon armed citizens for the purpose of keeping peace (Kopel 2015). The historical origins of the Posse Comitatus can be traced back to ninth-century England at a time when citizen involvement in policing matters was mandated by law (much like jury duty) (Kopel 2015). With the development of formalized police agencies, the need for citizens to act in this role has significantly diminished.

Vigilante-oriented Posse Comitatus groups emerged in the 70s. These groups were small and decentralized but anarchistic in nature and sometimes engaged in violent acts. Adherents tended to be a mix of antigovernment, anti-tax, survivalist, conspiracy-oriented, Christian Identity anti-Semitists, individuals (Loeser 2015; Toy n.d.). Two main ideas underlay the Posse movement: (1) at one time, an ideal form of government existed in the U.S. that had no laws and did not mandate paying taxes; (2) and that a powerful conspiracy has gradually replaced this idealistic form of government with an illegitimate one, and by opposing the current government it is possible to reestablish the early legitimate government it (Pitcavage n.d.).

The Posse members utilized a number of strategies to oppose the illegitimate government, many of which are commonly used by sovereign citizens today. For instance, Posse members used pseudolegal arguments to fight against the federal government for impeding on what they considered their God-given individual rights (Loeser 2015). They believe that one should follow God's laws, as opposed to the laws created by man. One way to achieve that goal was to follow the "common law" (Pitcavage n.d.). Among Posse members, common law was the highest law of the land. It was derived from the Bible and in their antiquated view, it was unwritten and thus can be subjectively interpreted to suit the needs of Posse members. Pitcavage (n.d.) identified the following most frequently espoused common law beliefs among posse members, many of which have been adopted by sovereign citizens:

1. commonlaw cannot be modified by any legislator or court;
2. property rights cannot be controlled or taken away by the government;
3. the belief in jury nullification which essentially states that a jury can reject laws if they believe them to be unjust (Niewert 2016);
4. unless there is an injured party, no legal action is merited; *The Common Law Handbook For Juror's, Sherriff's, Bailiff's and Justice's* states the following on the first page of the book: "…The question each jurist must ask himself is, "Is there an injured party"? There is a Common Law principle which states that for there to be a crime, there must *first* be a victim (*corpus delecti*); the state cannot be the injured party. In the absence of a victim there can be no crime."; and,
5. an individual may assume the right to unrestricted action, including traveling without regulation or interference from the government.

Posse members were often involved in paramilitary training and used "paper terrorism" tactics, some of which included: suing the Federal Reserve, filing false liens against public officials, and the practice of "severation," which involves attempting to reclaim sovereignty or "true freedom" by returning or destroying driver licenses, Social Security cards and other government issued documents (Loeser 2015). Other Posse tactics involved establishing common law courts, attempting to impanel citizen grand juries, "indicting" public officials or serving them with nonbinding warrants (Federal Bureau of Investigation 1997), and the creation of "townships" in which people could ignore state and federal laws (Valeri and Borgeson 2018). Though Posse groups were largely curtailed after a member killed two federal marshals in 1983, elements of the Posse doctrine live on in the sovereign citizen movement.

1.3 The Militia Movement

There are great similarities among many of the aforementioned movements and the militia movement which gained strength in the 1990s. The militia movement refers to a loosely connected group of individuals engaged in paramilitary activities and who self-identified as belonging to a militia group (Pitcavage 2001). A common belief among militia members was that the U.S. government has negatively shifted away from the model of government intended by the founders in the eighteenth century (Jackson 2019). They too, much like posse members and sovereign citizens, contend that the government was increasingly tyrannical in nature and "good Americans" must protect themselves (with arms if necessary) against the government to defend their God-given rights (Jackson 2019).

A series of incidents were said to have contributed to the growth the militia movement. They include the Los Angeles riots (in response to the Rodney King verdict), and the exactment of the Brady Handgun Violence Prevention Act which mandated a five-day waiting period before an individual could obtain a firearms license (Bureau of Alcohol, Tobacco, Firearms and Explosives 2019), the passing of the federal assault weapons ban in 1994 under Democratic President Bill Clinton (Jackson 2019) and most especially, standoffs at Ruby Ridge, Idaho in 1992 and in Waco, Texas 1993 (Pitcavage 2001). While those incidents inspired some people to join the movement, Pitcavage (2001) argues that the true catalyst was the development of a patriot media network, which allowed for the easy spread and exchange of information. Pitcavage (2001) also believes that the greater acceptance of conspiracy theories also played a role, as well as the increasing antigovernment messaging among the National Rifle Association (NRA) who feared that the government was plotting to confiscate their firearms.

Some militia members were especially violent. Two high profile actors, Timothy McVeigh and Terry Nichols, placed a bomb inside a Ryder truck outside the Alfred P. Murrah Federal building in Oklahoma City on April 19, 1995. The explosion was responsible for the death of 168 people and injured an additional 700 more (Perliger and Sweeney 2019). The attack served as a double-edged sword for militia groups. On one hand, it placed a spotlight on militia groups. Lawmakers quickly acted to limit their activities (Perliger and Sweeney 2019). On the other hand, the new focus served to highlight their existence and in doing so, inadvertently helped to recruit new members. By 1996, the movement began to weaken after the government began prosecuting and ultimately incarcerating various high-profile militia members (Pitcavage 2001).

It is important to note that while Terry Nichols is considered a member of the militia/patriot movement, he is also a well-known sovereign citizen (Federal Bureau of Investigation 2011). He, like other sovereigns, rejects the legitimacy of the government. He would refer to himself as a "nonresident alien (Rimer 1995)." He wrote letters to authorities renouncing his citizenship indicating that: "I no longer am a citizen of the corrupt political corporate state of Michigan and the United States of America … I follow the Common Law, not the Uniform Commercial Codes,

Michigan statutes, etc., that are all colorable laws… I lawfully "squarely challenge" the fraudulent usurping octopus of JURISDICTION/AUTHORITY (cited in Item #2) which does not apply to me... It is therefore now mandatory for… [the]so-called "IRS", for example, to prove its jurisdiction" (The Lectric Law Library n.d.). In court proceedings, he would defy judicial orders, holler at judges and claim that he was "a layman, a natural person, a common law citizen under threat of duress in the challenge of the jurisdiction of the court" (The Lectric Law Library n.d.). He and his brother were also known to mark paper money with a red stamp indicating they did not accept its validity (Maraniss and Pincus 1995). They would also refuse to buy license plates for their vehicles and register their cars, common sovereign citizen tactics.

The militia movement saw a resurgence in 2008 because of two main factors: the economic recession and the election of America's first black president, Barack Obama (Beckett 2019). An increase in the number of threats coincided with President Obama winning the Democratic nomination (Beckett 2019). Recruiting efforts centered upon generating fear and paranoia about having an African American Democrat running the country (Beckett 2019). Smear campaigns involved painting President Obama as being a secret Muslim, and not a U.S. citizen (Beckett 2019). Tea party rallies and far-right conservatives complained about government excess (Jackson 2019). In 2013, hundreds of antigovernment supporters, with guns, from around the country, traveled to Bunkerville, Nevada to support rancher Cliven Bundy and his family who were involved in an armed standoff with the government over his refusal to pay more than one million dollars in grazing fees (Levin 2018). The end of the standoff came after the federal government retreated in an effort to avoid violence.

In 2016, the fight with the government was reignited when two of Cliven's Bundy's sons, along with a number of supporters, engaged in an armed occupation of the Malheur National Wildlife Refuge. The Bundy's were spurred to action in support of the Hammonds, father and son ranchers, who had been sentenced to prison for arson on federal land (and who were eventually pardoned by President Trump) (Sullivan and Turkewitz 2018). After more than 40 days of occupation, they and their supporters were arrested; one occupier was shot by the federal government (Jackson 2019). A judge eventually dismissed many of the charges against Bundy and his sons, emboldening militia members in their fight for what they consider an overreaching federal government (Levin 2018). Two of Cliven's sons, Ryan and Ammon, both heavily involved in the armed standoffs, were acquitted in federal court (Coffman 2018). Ryan Bundy, a self-identified sovereign citizen, once filed a motion with the U.S. district court attempting to separate himself from U.S. laws. His motion indicated that he was declaring himself "a sovereign citizen of the Bundy society" (Haas 2018). Within the lengthy filing, which includes over 95 "facts" about himself and his relationship with the government and God, he declared himself "a creation of God rather than a person as defined by legal dictionaries" and thus not subject to laws (Haas 2018). Ryan was so emboldened by his "win" against the government that he ran for governor of Nevada in 2018. He was not elected.

1.4 Conclusion

This chapter explored the historical antecedents of various ideological groups who have influenced the modern-day sovereign citizen movement. Members self-proclaim an identity that has no official standing in the world. Their belief systems are devoid of any legitimate legal foundation. The typical sovereign citizen became one, in an attempt to escape prosecution for their illegal activities. Ultimately, sovereign citizens are motivated by self-interest and a desire to evade the law. Sovereign citizens present a unique threat to the American Society and as such deserve much more attention. Their core beliefs will be described in the next chapter.

References

Baker, P. (1986). IRS says nothing certain but death of tax-protesting. *Los Angeles Times*. p.OC_D1.

Beckett, L. (2019, August 8). "Blood on their hands": The intelligence officer whose warning over white supremacy was ignored. *The Guardian*. Retrieved from https://www.theguardian.com/us-news/2019/aug/07/white-supremacist-terrorism-intelligence-analyst

Berger, J. M. (2016). Without prejudice: What sovereign citizens believe. Washington D.C.: George Washington University. Washington, D.C. Retrieved from https://cchs.gwu.edu/sites/cchs.gwu.edu/files/downloads/Occasional%20Paper_Berger.pdf

Bureau of Alcohol, Tobacco, Firearms and Explosives. (2019). *Brady Law*. Retrieved from https://www.atf.gov/rules-and-regulations/brady-law

Coffman, K. (2018. March 8). States' rights rancher Ryan Bundy to run for Nevada governor. *Reuters*. Retrieved from https://www.reuters.com/article/us-nevada-election-bundy/states-rights-rancher-ryan-bundy-to-run-for-nevada-governor-idUSKCN1GL06E

Federal Bureau of Investigation. (1997). *Terrorism in the United States 1997*. Washington, DC: Federal Bureau of Investigation, Counterterrorism Threat Assessment and Warning Unit, National Security Division.

Federal Bureau of Investigation. (2011). *Sovereign citizens: A growing domestic threat to law enforcement*. Washington, DC: Federal Bureau of Investigation, Counterterrorism Division. Retrieved from https://leb.fbi.gov/articles/featured-articles/sovereign-citizens-a-growing-domestic-threat-to-law-enforcement.

Haas, R. (2018, July 28). Ryan Bundy declares himself "idiot" not subject to US courts. *Oregon Public Broadcasting*. Retrieved from https://www.opb.org/news/series/burns-oregon-standoff-bundy-militia-news-updates/ryan-bundy-incompetent-subject-federal-law/

Jackson, S. (2019). Nullification through armed civil disobedience: A case study of strategic framing in the patriot/militia movement. *Dynamics of Asymmetric Conflict, 12*(1), 90–109. https://doi.org/10.1080/17467586.2018.1563904.

Kopel, D. B. (2015). The *Posse Comitatus* and the office of sheriff: Armed citizens summoned to the aid of law enforcement. *The Journal of Criminal Law & Criminology, 104*(4), 761–850. doi: 0091-4169/15/10404-0761.

Levin, S. (2018, January 8). Stunning victory for Bundy family as all charges dismissed in 2014 standoff case. *The Guardian*. Retrieved from https://www.theguardian.com/us-news/2018/jan/08/bundy-family-charges-dropped-nevada-armed-standoff

Levitas, D. (2001). Tracing the opposition to taxes in America. *Southern Poverty Law Center*. Retrieved from https://www.splcenter.org/fighting-hate/intelligence-report/2001/tracing-opposition-taxes-america

Loeser, C. E. (2015). From paper terrorists to cop killers: The sovereign citizen threat. *North Carolina Law Review., 93*(4), 1106–1139. Retrieved from http://scholarship.law.unc.edu/cgi/viewcontent.cgi?article=4744&context.

Marasniss, D., & Pincus, D. W. (1995, April 30). Putting the pieces together. *Washington Post*. Retrieved from https://www.washingtonpost.com/archive/politics/1995/04/30/putting-the-pieces-together/f081925f-e483-4e21-89da-a18884558eca/

Neiwert, D. (2016, April 7). The uncomfortable link between jury empowerment and bigotry. *Washington Post*. Retrieved from https://www.washingtonpost.com/news/in-theory/wp/2016/04/07/the-uncomfortable-link-between-jury-empowerment-and-bigotry/

Perliger, A., & Sweeney, M. M. (2019). Terrorism: Domestic. In L. R. Shapiro & M.-H. Maras (Eds.), *Encyclopedia of Security and Emergency Management* (pp. 1–9). https://doi.org/10.1007/978-3-319-69891-5_250-1.

Pitcavage, M. (2001). Camouflage and conspiracy: The militia movement from Ruby Ridge to Y2K. *American Behavioral Scientist, 44*(6), 957–981. https://doi.org/10.1177/00027640121956610.

Pitcavage, M. (n.d.). *Sons of the posse: The resurgence of the extreme right in America*. Unpublished manuscript.

Porth, V. (1971). The Hon. George Templar and the United States of America, 453 F.2d 330.

Rimer, S. (1995). With extremism and explosives, a drifting life found a purpose. *The New York Times*. p.1.

Semerad, T. (1995, May 28). Tax-protest movement getting bigger, bolder. *The Salt Lake Tribune*, pp. A16.

Sullivan, E., & Turkewitz, J. (2018, July 10). Trump pardons Oregon ranchers whose case inspired wildlife refuge takeover. *The New York Times*. Retrieved from https://www.nytimes.com/2018/07/10/us/politics/trump-pardon-hammond-oregon.html

The Lectric Law Library. (n.d.). 992–93 *Nichol's Documents Submitted As Evidence By Gov't 7/96 Re Suppression Of Evidence Issues*. Retrieved from https://www.lectlaw.com/files/case42.htm

The New York Times. (2008, April 25). Wesley Snipes gets 3 years for not filing tax returns. *The New York Times*. Retrieved from https://www.nytimes.com/2008/04/25/business/25snipes.html

Toy, E. (n.d.). Posse Comitatus. In *The Oregon Encyclopedia*. Retrieved from https://oregonencyclopedia.org/articles/posse_comitatus/#.XY4L9UZKjzn.

Valeri, R. M., & Borgeson (Eds.). (2018). *Terrorism in America*. New York, NY: Routledge.

Chapter 2
Behavior and Underlying Ideology

Chapter two will explore the unusual belief systems of sovereign citizens. Their belief system can be diverse and although there are differences between the behaviors and tactics of sovereign citizens, their core beliefs remain the same. A description of those common themes and core beliefs is presented below.

The label of "sovereign citizen" is given to persons who share specific core beliefs. Those who call themselves sovereign citizens do so without having been officially recognized by any government agency. There is no official licensing board or government certifying agency. Anyone can self-identify as a sovereign citizen but if they do not possess the core beliefs of a sovereign citizen, they would not be labeled as a sovereign citizen. Likewise, someone who denies being a sovereign citizen, would nonetheless be considered a sovereign citizen if they possessed the core beliefs of a sovereign citizen.

This collection of core beliefs identifies a group of persons. It is not the label of "sovereign citizen" that is of importance. It is the group of shared beliefs which identifies the sovereign citizen. Persons who share these same core beliefs are commonly labeled by the police, by the courts and by the press, as "sovereign citizens." The individuals so labeled, may call themselves by other names, such as "free person," "free man on the land," "natural man," "living person," "flesh-and-blood human being," "natural citizen," "sovereign man," and by other names. Regardless of the names with which they self-identify, they share the same fundamental beliefs concerning the government. They believe the U.S. government is illegitimate. They believe that they are immune to all of the laws of the U.S. government and are immune to arrest and conviction.

This book is primarily concerned with the sovereign citizen movement in the U.S. of America and will focus on sovereign citizens in the U.S. while acknowledging the fact that sovereign citizens exist in most democratic countries around the

---

The original version of this chapter was revised. The correction to this chapter is available at https://doi.org/10.1007/978-3-030-45851-5_8

© The Author(s), under exclusive license to Springer Nature Switzerland AG 2020, Corrected Publication 2020
C. M. Sarteschi, *Sovereign Citizens*, SpringerBriefs in Psychology, https://doi.org/10.1007/978-3-030-45851-5_2

world. The next chapter will discuss the origins of these beliefs. This chapter will list and discuss the beliefs themselves.

Perhaps the most important belief, which underlies many of the other beliefs, is the illegitimacy of the American government. Sovereign citizens see the U.S. government as an elaborate conspiracy foisted upon the American people. They believe that the government has no power to make laws or enforce laws. They believe that the government is run in secrecy and is well aware of its own illegitimacy. It is the secrecy of the government that allows it to impose its power upon the people. Once an individual can pierce through this veil of secrecy, then the individual is immune to the power of the government. Once the sovereign citizen realizes that the American government is just an illusion, then the sovereign citizen no longer has to pay taxes, obtain a driver's license, register their vehicles, obey laws or follow the commands of police officers. They believe that neither the police or the courts have jurisdiction over them and at traffic stops and while in the courtroom, they vociferously demand that the officer or judge show them proof of their jurisdiction. The sovereign citizens conduct at a traffic stop or in the courtroom, ranges from animated arguing, to violence. Sovereign citizens are certain, beyond a shadow of a doubt, that they have figured out the conspiracy. The police have no power over them and neither do the courts. The sovereign citizen is annoyed and angry at the police officer and the judge for knowingly carrying on this scam. The sovereign citizen is neither patient or respectful. Instead, their behavior is disrespectful, angry, condescending, aggressive and often violent. Many sovereign citizens, after having been stopped for a traffic violation, have been pepper sprayed, tased, thrown to the ground, handcuffed and arrested. Some encounters have led to the death of the officer, the sovereign citizen or both.

Ironically, though the sovereign citizen does not believe in the legitimacy of the U.S. government, they claim to believe in the legitimacy of the Constitution of the U.S. However, it is only their very unique interpretation of the Constitution that they will accept. The judicially proven interpretation of the Constitution, the one with which we have lived since the adoption of the Constitution, is vehemently denied by the sovereign citizen. Sovereign citizens will take words and phrases from the Constitution, to support their belief that American laws do not apply to them. In addition, though they believe themselves to be above all of the laws with which we live, they will often take words and phrases, from our existing laws, splice them together in an attempt to prove that U.S. laws do not apply to them. When stopped by police officers or when appearing in court, the sovereign citizen will recite laws and Supreme Court case findings.

2.1 Jurisdiction

At traffic stops and in court, often the first tactic of the sovereign citizen is to demand that the police officer or the judge prove jurisdiction over them. After all, if the police officer or judge does not have jurisdiction, the traffic stop must end or the case must be thrown out of court. It is the assumption of the sovereign citizen that neither the police officer or judge can prove jurisdiction, since the sovereign citizen's interpretation of the Constitution does not allow for them to have jurisdiction and thus the jurisdiction issue amounts to a "get out of jail free card." In the many cases reviewed by this research, the jurisdiction tactic has never worked. No police officer has allowed a sovereign citizen to leave a traffic stop after having been reminded, that they did not have jurisdiction over the sovereign citizen. No judge, to the full extent of this research, has ever thanked the sovereign citizen for reminding them that they had no jurisdiction over the sovereign citizen and thus greatly appreciated the prevention of a miscarriage of justice. The sovereign citizen jurisdiction tactic has never worked. Police officers and judges enforce the existing laws of the U.S. of America. No exclusion is made for persons claiming to be sovereign citizens. Citizens in this country, visitors to this country, and noncitizens who live in this country, are all equally subject to the law. There are no exclusions.

Many times, at a traffic stop, a sovereign citizen will refuse to cooperate with the police officer, unless the police officer first proves jurisdiction. The sovereign citizen demands more than simple verbal proof. They demand written proof, to be shown to them. No police officer has ever supplied the sovereign citizen with written proof of jurisdiction. It is the belief of the sovereign citizen, with their unique interpretation of the Constitution and Supreme Court rulings, that the police officer or judge has no jurisdiction over them. Thus, it would be impossible to provide the written proof of jurisdiction. Nonetheless, asking for written proof is a standard weapon in the sovereign citizen arsenal.

2.2 Warrants

The sovereign citizen believes that they may only be pulled over by a police officer, if the police officer has a court issued warrant for their arrest. The sovereign citizen will refuse to cooperate with the police officer unless they are shown the physical warrants issued by the court for his arrest. Obviously, a written warrant is not necessary for a traffic stop.

2.3 Joinder

The sovereign citizen is very careful to resist the officer throughout the traffic stop, and during the subsequent arrest, should it occur. Similarly, in the courtroom, the sovereign citizen refuses to comply with the normal procedures, policies and rules of the court. In all the instances mentioned above, the sovereign citizen does so, so as not to engage in joinder. The sovereign citizen believes that legally they are immune to the laws of the U.S. with one dangerous exception, that of joinder. Joinder only occurs as a result of a mistake that was made in the speech or behavior of the sovereign citizen.

Joinder is a legal definition, which simply means that two or more legal matters are joined together and treated as a single legal matter. Sovereign citizens believe that they exist as two entities, the living breathing flesh-and-blood human and the fictitious legal entity, who possesses the same name and birth certificate as does the flesh-and-blood human. It is essential for the sovereign citizen to keep these two entities separate because legal authority only exists over the fictitious legal entity and not the flesh-and-blood human. The fictitious legal entity is referred to by the sovereign citizen as the "straw man." The straw man must not be joined to the flesh-and-blood man. If joinder does occur, then the flesh-and-blood man is subject to the same laws and punishments as is the straw man. Thus, joinder must be avoided at all costs by the sovereign citizen and their every word and action must be carefully planned so as not to engage in joinder.

2.4 I Do Not Consent

As already established, the sovereign citizen does not believe that the police or the courts have power over them. Since they belief that neither the courts or the police can enforce their will upon the sovereign citizen, the sovereign citizen must not make the mistake of consenting to the power of the police or the power of the courts. At traffic stops and while in court, the sovereign citizen makes it abundantly clear that they "do not consent." They do this in multiple ways, including by verbally repeating over and over that they do not consent. They do not consent to the traffic stop and tell this to the officer. They do not consent to any searches of their vehicle, even after being told that they are under arrest. They do not consent to being arrested and when told that they are under arrest, they commonly say "no, I am not under arrest." When told to exit their vehicles, they say "no." When told to unlock their doors, they say "no." When told to roll down the window, so that the officer can reach in to open the locked door, they say "no." Even when told that if they do not unlock the door or roll down the window, that the window will be broken and they will be dragged from the vehicle, they say "no." While the window is being broken and they are being dragged from the vehicle, they repeatedly scream "I do not consent, I do not consent." Often, traffic stops are recorded by the sovereign citizen as are court appearances, by hidden cameras. In both instances the video recordings, show the shock, amazement, and outrage displayed by the sovereign citizen when they find out that adherence to the law does not require their consent.

2.5 Traveling

When stopped by a police officer and told by the officer that they were driving too fast, or driving erratically, or driving in the wrong lane, the sovereign citizen immediately informs the officer that they were not "driving." When the police officer tells the sovereign citizen, he had tracked him on radar driving 20 miles over the speed limit, the sovereign citizen responds "I was not driving, I was traveling." When the police officer asks the sovereign citizen for his driver's license, the sovereign citizen responds "I don't need a driver's license." When the officer informs the sovereign citizen that everyone driving a motor vehicle in the U.S. is required to have a driver's license, the sovereign citizen responds "I was traveling, not driving." When the police officer tells the sovereign citizen that anyone operating a motor vehicle is required to have a driver's license, the sovereign citizen responds "this is not a motor vehicle. It is my personal property" or responds with "this is my personal conveyance and not an automobile or motor vehicle." The sovereign citizen refuses to admit that they are driving or that a driver's license is necessary. Since traveling is mentioned in the Constitution as a right of all citizens, of the U.S., the sovereign citizen feels that by simply denying that they are a driver or that their motorized vehicle is a vehicle, they then have no need to acquire a driver's license and cannot be punished for not having one.

The sovereign citizen will, at times, admit that a driver's license is necessary to drive but only if the driving is done for commercial purposes. They will tell the police officer that "he is not for hire" or that "no one is paying him to drive" and since he does not fit the definition of a commercial driver, he does not need a driver's license. Also, many sovereign citizens believe that returning their driver's license, by registered mail, to the states' Department of Motor Vehicles (DMV), effectively removes the "contract" that they have with the state. After removing their contractual agreement with the state, they believe that they are then free to travel without a driver's license. They also believe that the rules of the road, such as speed limits, no longer apply to them. They only apply to people with drivers' licenses who have agreed, by obtaining a license, to follow the laws that pertain to driving. They are free to make any lane change they want at any time. They are free to travel at whatever speed they desire. Stop signs are irrelevant and traffic lights have no meaning.

2.6 Refusing to Identify Themselves

Sovereign citizens will not only refuse to show the officer their driver's license, they will often refuse to show the officer any form of identification that would show their legal name. They may, however, offer homemade documents that identifies them with a new name, which they have created for themselves. Their goal is to hide their real identity. If the officer asks them to verbally identify themselves, they may simply refuse, saying "I don't answer questions." If asked for the name on their birth certificate, they will often say that since they were given that name at birth, they were too young to remember that name. They sometimes will say that they do not have a last name. For instance, they may say "I am Joe from the clan Smith." The sovereign citizen belief is that they do not have to provide their name to a police officer and if they do provide their name, they may be creating a contractual relationship with law enforcement. Again, the belief is that the police have no power over them, unless they make a mistake in their interaction with the police and inadvertently create a "contract" with the police. This contract will give the police power over them.

2.7 I Don't Answer Questions

Beyond refusing to answer questions about their identity, the sovereign citizen may refuse to answer any questions asked of them by the police. Is this your car? Is this car registered? Do you have insurance? May I see your driver's license? Do you have a weapon in the car? Can you roll your window down further? Do you have any warrants? To all of these and more, the sovereign citizen, simply replies "I don't answer questions."

2.8 Self-Made License Plates

Often, the sovereign citizen will have created their own license plates or might have ordered more official looking license plates from an internet website. These license plates may contain both letters and numbers or words. Often, the words used, will say something to the effect "not commercial" or "not for hire." The sovereign citizen's belief is that only commercial, for hire, persons need a driver's license. By stating clearly on the license plate that they are not commercial drivers, the sovereign citizen believes all the power of the police has been removed and they do not need to follow any laws that are applicable to "drivers." After all, they are travelers not drivers.

Though they steer a motorized vehicle down the highway at 70 miles an hour, a vehicle that the rest of the world would refer to as an automobile, car or truck, they are not "driving" and the thing in which they sit, is not an automobile a car or a truck. It is a "personal conveyance." They are "traveling" in a "personal conveyance" and the laws of the road only apply to drivers of automobiles, cars, and trucks, not "conveyances." To become a driver, one must be making money from driving the automobile. Thus, by clearly stating on the homemade license plate "not for hire" makes them immune to all laws and the police officers that enforce those laws.

2.9 Black's Law Dictionary

Sovereign citizens often cite Black's Law dictionary at traffic stops and when in the courtroom. This dictionary is asserted, by the sovereign citizen, to be the definitive determiner of U.S. law. In actuality, this dictionary has no legal authority or place in the American courtroom. It is no more than a dictionary of legal terms. As a dictionary it has no more legal authority than does Merriam-Webster's, Oxford or Collins. Black's Law dictionary is the basis for the arguments presented by sovereign citizens. The sovereign citizen will reference this dictionary, much as a licensed attorney would reference the U.S. Constitution or state and federal law.

2.10 What's the Emergency?

Often, when the sovereign citizen's is first approached by a police officer, at a traffic stop, the sovereign citizen says "what's the emergency officer?" They might also add "how may I be of assistance?" There is a basic belief among sovereign citizens that law enforcement officer may only use their flashing lights in an emergency situation. The sovereign citizen believes that the traffic stop is not an emergency situation and thus the law enforcement officers is breaking the law by using his flashing lights. Often, the sovereign citizen will reprimand the police officer for using their flashing lights.

2.11 Fee Schedules

Sovereign citizens will often threaten police officers with lawsuits. The idea is that the threat of a lawsuit will frighten off the police officer. The sovereign citizen makes it clear that he is suing not just the police department but is additionally, filing a personal lawsuit against the officer involved. As part of the lawsuit, the sovereign citizen includes their personal fee schedule. At the traffic stop, the printed fee schedule, will often be handed to the officer. It contains a list of fees that the sovereign citizen expects to be paid for their time and inconvenience. These amounts may be from thousands of dollars per hour to millions of dollars per day. Sometimes, these schedules also mandate the type of currency that will be accepted in payment. It is not unusual to demand that the fees be paid in gold or silver.

2.12 What's Your Bond Number?

Sovereign citizens believe that all police officers must be bonded. The bond is an insurance policy of sorts, that guarantees the money that would be paid to a claimant, should a police officer be found liable. Sovereign citizens will demand from the police officer a copy of his bond or his bond number. If the police officer is unable to provide proof of his bond, then the sovereign citizen believes the traffic stop is invalid and that the police officer must end the traffic stop and allow them to go free.

2.13 Do You Have a Business Card?

Sovereign citizens believe that a police officer must have three forms of identification. One of the three, must be a business card. Some police officers do carry business cards and when asked will give one to a sovereign citizen but many do not carry business cards. Without the business card, the sovereign citizen believes the officer has not adequately proven that they are a police officer and thus has no power as a police officer. When the officer fails to provide a business card, the response of the sovereign citizen will be to deny that the police officer is a police officer. Even when the sovereign citizen sees the police officer step out of a 4000-pound automobile, with flashing blue and red lights, and the words "police" painted in two-foot letters prominently upon every panel of the automobile, the sovereign citizen denies that this officer is an officer. Even though the individual claiming to be a police officer, looks completely like a police officer, with a name tag stating that they are a police officer, with a badge stating that they are a police officer, without a business card the sovereign citizen will deny that this individual is a police officer. Even when two other police cars arrive, all with appropriate emergency lights and appropriate markings, from which four police officers emerge to tell the sovereign citizen that indeed their detaining officer is a police officer, the sovereign citizen will accept nothing less than a "business card."

2.14 Recording Traffic Stops or Live Broadcasting

It is very common for sovereign citizens to record their interactions with police officers. Often, they will live broadcast their traffic stop to Facebook or YouTube. Doing so, will provide them with either video evidence or online witnesses to the behavior of the police officer. The core belief of the sovereign citizen is that law enforcement has no jurisdiction over them, so every part of the traffic stop and the role of the officer in that stop, is illegal. They will often inform the officer that tens of thousands of people will view their videos or are presently viewing the traffic stop. They repeatedly remind the officer that everything that the officer is doing is illegal and tell the officer that they will lose their job and be personally sued, unless the traffic stop immediately ends and the sovereign citizen may resume "traveling" down the highway, in his "personal conveyance."

2.15 Calling 911

Strangely, during a traffic stop, sovereign citizens will sometimes call 911 to ask for help. It would appear to make no sense, calling 911, to ask for police to help them from the same police who are conducting the traffic stop. Calling 911 will result in the dispatching of police officers and that would be the expected result of the call. Often, 911 operators are very confused when a sovereign citizen calls asking for police help and even more confused when the operator finds out that the police are at the scene already. It makes no sense to the 911 operator. In one case, a female sovereign citizen was running from a traffic stop and being chased by several police cars. She was traveling at excessively high speed, ignoring stop signs and traffic lights and ignoring the flashing lights and sirens that were directly behind her. She called 911 and told the operator to "call off the dogs." She talked to the operator while traveling at speeds in excess of 75 miles per hour, with police cars right behind her, lights flashing and sirens screaming. She told the operator that she would be suing for millions of dollars and all law enforcement involved, including the 911 operator, would be losing their jobs. The sovereign citizen, then made a magnanimous gesture and promised the 911 operator that she would forget about everything, if the 911 operator would "call off her dogs" and the police would end their chase. The 911 operator then told the sovereign citizen that she should immediately pull over and fully cooperate with the police officers. The sovereign citizen did eventually pull over and was immediately arrested. That call to 911, by a sovereign citizen, was in no way unique. Many other sovereign citizens have called 911 to complain that the police have stopped them and to ask the 911 operator to send police officers to end the traffic stop, by police officers. Of course, this maneuver makes no sense. The phone call by the sovereign citizen, is simply meant to document the traffic stop for a future lawsuit. The sovereign citizen knows that all 911 calls are recorded and kept. The sovereign citizen believes the recorded phone call will be helpful in future legal action against the police department.

2.16 Return Driver's License

Remember, sovereign citizens were not always sovereign citizens. There was a time when they followed the laws of the U.S. Following the laws of the country, most sovereign citizens had acquired a driver's license, at some point in their life. This presents a problem for sovereign citizens because they believe that the driver's license itself equates to a contract between themselves and the U.S. government. This contract means that they must now follow the laws pertaining to driving on all public roads and highways. In their minds, they have made the most grievous of all mistakes, they have entered into "contract." They cannot rewrite history but if they could, they would never have gotten a driver's license in the first place. They have a driver's license. The mistake has already been made. They are under contract. That means that the police do have control over them. That means that they can be arrested. That means that they have to follow the speed limits. That means that their driver's license can be suspended or taken away completely. They have no impunity. They cannot drive 100 miles per hour in a 45 mile per hour zone. They must stop at stop signs. They have to reduce their speed to 15 miles per hour when passing a school. They cannot pass another car in a no passing zone. They must follow all the rules of the road, just as all other American drivers must do, and that is something that sovereign citizens just do not want to do.

Fortunately, sovereign citizens have a fix for this problem. They need to renounce their driver's license. By doing so, they break their contract with the state. Some sovereign citizens think that it is as simple as putting their driver's license in an envelope and sending it to the DMV. Others, try to make it more official by calling the DMV and telling the operator that they want to break all contracts with the DMV. Of course, the operator is at a complete loss as to the procedure for "breaking all contracts" and tells the sovereign citizen just that. The sovereign citizen will often hang up and then redial and speak to a different operator. Since no operator can help them, with a procedure that does not exist, they then begin a laborious process of moving from one supervisor to the supervisor's, supervisor. The sovereign citizen may also create a "legal" document, breaking their "contracts" with the state's DMV. This document consists of nothing more than a simple written statement expressing the desire of the sovereign citizen to have all contracts, between them and the state, dissolved. How does this statement become a legal document? In the mind of the sovereign citizen, it becomes a legally binding document by going to a notary and having the notary stamp applied to it. For good measure, the conscientious sovereign citizen will then send the document by registered or certified mail. Granted, it does take a little time to write the document and may cost them a few dollars to mail it but that is a small price to pay for never again having to follow any traffic law and to gain complete immunity from the police.

2.17 Revoking the Vehicle's Registration

Before becoming a sovereign citizen, while the individual was living as a law-abiding citizen, it is likely that their vehicles were registered, and that was a mistake. Once again, joinder had occurred. At least in the mind of the sovereign citizen, it had. The plates were a mistake. The sovereign should never have gotten plates in the first place but now that the mistake has been made, it must be rectified. It is not enough to allow your plates to expire or to just ignore the letter from the state telling you that your plates are about to expire, because joinder is currently in effect. Joinder, must be broken. Removing your plates from the vehicle, is not enough. The mistake was the original registration. In the minds of sovereign citizens, there is a difference between a "never" registered vehicle and an unregistered vehicle. A "never" registered vehicle is just fine and never needs plates when driving on the roads of America. But a previously registered, but currently not registered vehicle, presents problems of joinder. The sovereign citizen had stupidly, before having acquired the wisdom of sovereign citizen-hood, created joinder with the state. The sovereign citizen cannot ignore the registration renewal letter because by previously registering the vehicle, they are contractually obligated to continually reregister the vehicle. There is a solution to this problem. The plates must be physically returned to the DMV or sent by registered mail. A notarized letter must accompany the plates and additional letters also must be sent to appropriate officials across the state. These officials may range from the employee at the window of the DMV, to the governor of the state. Once the "T's" have been crossed and the "I's" have been dotted, complete immunity from the police, all traffic laws and the cost of yearly vehicle registration will be obtained. Not bad, for a little time and some postage.

2.18 Not U.S. Citizens

Sovereign citizens make it abundantly clear that they are not U.S. citizens. Their thinking is that only U.S. citizens are required to follow the laws of the U.S. Of course, this is not true. If it were true, visitors from other countries could rob banks, kill whomever they choose and all without consequence. Even if caught, they could not be arrested and the police could do no more than to politely asked them to "stop doing it."

Sovereigns citizens, could not be more wrong on this point. The laws of the U.S. apply to everyone within the borders of the U.S. No exceptions allowed. Citizens of virtually any country one could think of, are currently incarcerated in American jails and prisons. More importantly, many sovereign citizens are currently incarcerated in U.S. prisons and jails, with sentences running from just a few days, up to life without the possibility of parole.

The sovereign citizen's argument that they do not have to follow the laws of the U.S. because they are not a U.S. citizen, is blatantly false. As a possible remedy, which would require the passage of new laws, when a sovereign citizen tells a police officer or a judge that they are not a citizen of the U.S. they would be taken at their word. When they emphatically and repeatedly declare that they are not citizens of the U.S., they then would be immediately, but courteously, driven to the nearest airport.

Have Congress pass any necessary laws, to make that possible, then let's see how much a "not a citizen of the U.S," enjoys being a "not a citizen" of some other country. Let us respect the sovereign citizen. Let's not force them to be American citizens, if they do not wish to be.

When the sovereign citizen denounces their U.S. citizenship, the outcome should be either a courteous wave goodbye, as we escort them to their departing airplane, or a friendly wave of hello, when the sovereign citizen enters the gates of our prison system.

2.19 Driving Is a God-Given Right

Sovereign citizens assert that no man-made law can limit the rights given by God, to them. Sovereigns citizens also maintain that the American Constitution similarly guarantees their right to travel upon all roads and highways. The Constitution does allow for free travel between states. The Constitution also allows for each state to make its own laws. Every state, in the union, has made its own laws concerning driving vehicles upon the public roadways. The laws in each state vary to some degree but are remarkably similar. All states require a valid driver's license. All states maintain that driving is a privilege and not a right. Drivers licenses may be suspended or revoked, in which case an individual may not operate a motor vehicle on any public roadway. Sovereigns believe that the state laws regarding driving are not valid, since no law can limit the rights given them by the Constitution. Sovereign citizens find all state laws, regarding driving, to be unconstitutional.

This disagreement is not simply a matter of opinion. It is a matter of legality. The validity of law is tested all the time and that testing takes place in the Supreme Court of the U.S. The Supreme Court has ruled on many occasions that state laws requiring driver's licenses are valid and constitutional. Though the Supreme Court is the highest court of the land its rulings are not sufficient for the sovereign citizen. Sovereigns, in their minds, have appealed the Supreme Court's rulings to a higher court, the court of God. Apparently, they believe God has ruled in their favor. However, I seriously doubt they have written paperwork to prove it.

2.20 Not a Car, Truck or Vehicle

There is a basic tenet in philosophy. "As a thing acts, so it is." Sometimes, this idea is presented more simply in popular culture. "If it walks like a duck, quacks like a duck, it is a duck." The basic idea here, is that it does not matter what you call something, it is what it is. It does not matter what you call your dog, it is still a dog. You can call your dog a lion, or a horse, or an eagle but if it acts like a dog, walks like a dog, and barks like a dog, it is a dog. In an attempt to circumvent the motor vehicle laws, sovereign citizens go to great lengths to never refer to their vehicle with any language that could possibly sound like the language used in motor vehicle laws. When told by a police officer that his car was traveling 60 miles per hour in a 25 mile per hour zone, the sovereign citizen will reply "officer, this is not a car." When the officer changes their language and says "your automobile was tracked at 60 miles per hour in a 25 mile per hour zone." The sovereign citizen will reply "but officer this is not an automobile." When the officer changes their language, to include the widest possible frame of reference, and says "motor vehicle," you guessed it, the sovereign citizen says "but officer this is not a motor vehicle."

During this whole exchange between police officer and sovereign citizen, the police officer is being patient and explanatory, trying to help what they believe to be a confused motorist. On the other hand, the sovereign citizen is becoming more frustrated and angry. They become more impatient, the longer they are delayed. They will often berate the police officer and chastise them for not knowing "the law." The police officers, still trying to help what they consider to be a "confused motorist," will try to explain the most easily grasped, "this is a motor vehicle, it has a motor and it moves. Thus, this is a motor vehicle and all motor vehicle laws apply." The sovereign citizen will simply say "this is not a motor vehicle." There is no explanation given as to why the sovereign citizen denies the officers' explanation of a motor vehicle. Eventually, the sovereign citizen will explain to the police officer, what the name of the thing is, in which they sit and steer, as they drive down our American roads and highways. It is not a car, a truck an SUV or an automobile, it is a "personal conveyance."

Sovereign citizens may choose not to refer to the thing in which they sit, as a personal conveyance. They may choose to refer to it as a "household good." In the mind of the sovereign citizen, motor vehicle laws do not apply to "household goods," or "personal conveyances." By renaming the thing in which they sit, a sovereign citizen believes they are now above the law. They have found a clever loophole, such that they need not follow the rules of the road, they need not register their automobile nor secure for themselves a driver's license. Most importantly, the sovereign citizen has achieved complete impunity from the law.

All of this, achieved by simply renaming their motor vehicle "a personal conveyance" or "a household good." Each state has laws governing motor vehicles. It is obvious that these laws pertain to all vehicles, which have motors and travel on public roadways.

A vehicle is something that is used to transport something. That something can be a person or a box, or food, or a load of television sets. That is a vehicle. Now, does it have a motor? A motor is the device that propels the vehicle. This motor could be gasoline, diesel, electric, or anything else that provides propulsion.

It is pretty simple and blatantly obvious. If it is a vehicle and it has a motor, it is a motor vehicle and all motor vehicle laws apply. The sovereign citizen may choose to call it a personal conveyance or a household good but their personal conveyance or household good meets every legal definition of a motor vehicle. Yet, they deny it is a motor vehicle. What do you think? Is a car or truck or an SUV, a motor vehicle? Of course, it is. To think otherwise would be indicative of a delusional disorder. In fact, many sovereign citizens, who espouse this type of rhetoric in court, are court ordered to have a psychiatric evaluation. To aggressively and insistently contend that your car, which was just stopped by a police officer, is not a motor vehicle, is enough to have a judge order that a psychiatrist determine your sanity. Renaming their car or truck a "personal conveyance," will not protect the sovereign citizen. Calling that big, bright, yellow, thing in the sky, "the moon," will not protect a sovereign citizen from sunburn. A motor vehicle by any other name, is still a motor vehicle.

2.21 Corpus Delicti

In the courtroom or at a traffic stop, it is common for the sovereign citizen to ask "where is the corpus delicti?" The general meaning of corpus delicti is that a crime must have evidence of having been committed. It is not enough for someone to accuse you of a crime, of which you may or may not be guilty. Your guilt is a secondary consideration. First, there needs to be evidence of a crime. If your neighbor accuses you of killing your friend, you will not be arrested until there is sufficient evidence indicating that your friend is actually dead. Your neighbor's accusations are not enough. Often, no arrest will be made until your friend's body is found. However, finding your friend's body is not the only evidence that is acceptable. Perhaps, your friend's body will never be found. Perhaps, you dumped the body 50 miles out to sea and the body was quickly consumed by swarming sharks. No body does not mean no arrest. A luminol blood test performed by the police, may show a trail of blood leading from your kitchen to the garage door of your home. Luminol makes invisible bloodstains, visible. Forensic tests prove this blood to be your friend's. This evidence, along with the accusation made by your neighbor, should be enough to get you arrested by the police. The police now have sufficient evidence that your friend was murdered, that a crime was committed. Corpus delicti, means evidence that a crime was committed. Now, that the police have evidence that your friend was murdered, they need to find additional evidence to determine who is guilty of the murder.

One must remember, that an arrest is not a conviction. The observations of a police officer, are sufficient to produce an arrest. Innocent people, are arrested every day. The idea that innocent people may be arrested, is baked into the system. That is why all arrested people "are presumed to be innocent, until proven guilty in a court of law." There was a time in history, when all arrested people were presumed to be guilty and it was up to the arrested individual to prove their innocence. That change, is indeed a very big difference. Historically, it was up to the individual to prove their innocence. Now, it is up to the prosecuting attorney to prove the guilt of the arrested individual. The individual is not burdened with proving innocence. In fact, in our court system, no one is ever found to be innocent. When the foreman of the jury reads the verdict of the jury, they never say we find the accuser innocent of the charges. They say "we find the accused, guilty or not guilty." No one ever says the word, "innocent."

Corpus delicti means sufficient evidence. It means sufficient evidence to perform an arrest. It has nothing to do with guilt or innocence. When a police officer hears gunfire and the screams of murder coming from a bank building and then sees you running from the bank, gun in hand, carrying a large sack of money, it is likely that he will arrest you. It is the professional, trained observation of the police officer, that you are a murderous bank robber. But remember, they did not see you shoot anyone. They did not see you point a gun at the teller and take the large bag of money, that you hold in your hand. The only evidence that they have is you are the person running from the bank, holding a gun and a large sack of money. You may be the bank robber or you may be innocent. You might be a bank teller, chasing the actual robber, with your gun drawn, having picked up one of the sacks of money dropped by the actual robber.

Innocent people are arrested. The observations of the police officer are sufficient evidence for the arrest. When sovereign citizens cry "where is the corpus delicti," they are really saying "where is the proof of my guilt." It is not the job of the police officer to prove guilt. That is the job of the prosecuting attorney. The case is not being tried on the side of the road, nor should it be. The corpus delicti is simply the judgment of the police officer. No other evidence is needed. If the officer is correct in their judgment, someone is prosecuted. If they are wrong, in their judgment, the charges against the arrested individual, will be dropped at a later date or they will be found "not guilty" in a court of law.

At a traffic stop, corpus delicti is always present. Corpus delicti, is no more than the judgment of the police officer. The sovereign citizen, has already answered their own question, when they ask the police officer "where's the corpus delicti?" It is the officer they are talking to.

2.22 Where Is the Injured Party?

When it comes to traffic stops, sovereign citizens believe that they have many arguments to offer the officer, any one of which invalidates all power that the police may have over them. Various arguments are offered, by the sovereign citizen, and a common one is "where is the injured party?" In the mind of the sovereign citizen, traffic infractions of any kind are not crimes and the police officer only has power over them when crimes are involved. In the mind of the sovereign citizen, crimes can only occur when an individual is harmed in some way. No harm, no crime. Thus, when stopped by a police officer, the sovereign citizen will often say to the officer "where is the injured party?" In the mind of the sovereign citizen, they can quickly clear up the traffic stop and go on their way by simply determining if there is an injured party, claiming that they were harmed by the sovereign citizen. Police officers are seldom equipped to deal with the nonsensical, illogical rhetoric and behavior of the sovereign citizen. The words and reasoning of sovereign citizens make sense only to sovereign citizens. The police officer is ill-prepared, ill-equipped, to understand the invalid arguments and illogical reasoning of the sovereign citizen. It is the police officer's job, to be polite, explanatory and respectful of the person who is being detained. They are expected to show patience. In an attempt to do these things, they will try to explain to the sovereign citizen what the law is and where the sovereign citizen is incorrect in their thinking. The police officer does not know that they are talking to a sovereign citizen. They think that are talking to any normal motorist, who might actually be incomplete in their thinking about valid traffic laws. The police officer does not realize that they are talking to a sovereign citizen, who is in essence living in a different world of false assumptions and misinterpretations of the law.

When the police officer attempts to provide clarification and reassurance to the sovereign citizen, they are doomed to failure. They and the sovereign citizen are speaking two different languages. They believe in two different legal realities. The police officer has stopped the sovereign citizen under the current laws of the U.S. The sovereign citizen does not live under the current laws of the U.S. The police officer feels that reason and patience will clarify the situation. But they are doing no more than arguing the law with the sovereign citizen. They are explaining nothing. There can be no reasoning, where there is no common ground. The officer says that they do have power to enforce a traffic stop. This just angers the sovereign citizen, in an escalating manner.

The sovereign citizen believes that they may only be stopped by a police officer if there is "an injured party." The police officer knows better. Debating the law with a sovereign citizen, is a mistake. In their world, they are always right and no amount of arguing will change their mind. Licensed lawyers, debate the law in front of a judge. The judge or the jury, will determine guilt or not. The appellate court will determine the correctness of the decisions of the lower court and the Supreme Court will determine the validity of the law. Arguments between a police officer and a sovereign citizen, on the side of the road, will do nothing to determine the validity of a law.

Everyone driving on U.S. roads, is subject to the laws of the road. We all accept this but sovereign citizens do not. When the sovereign citizen explains to the police officer that they may only be stopped, if they have injured someone, how should the officer respond? Should they say "thank you, for correcting me. I guess they had that one wrong at the police academy. Have a nice day." There is nothing that the officer may say which would resolve the disagreement between them and the sovereign citizen. They are both living in different worlds, with different laws. The officers' patience and attempts at resolution, will be met with frustration, anger and exacerbation by the sovereign citizen.

Normal traffic stops do not involve injuries. There is no injured party when receiving a speeding ticket. One might argue that everyone in the state is an injured party whenever someone speeds or drives recklessly but that is insufficient for a sovereign citizen. The abstract "everyone" is not a flesh-and-blood-being and there must be damage to a flesh-and-blood-being for a police officer to have jurisdiction over a sovereign citizen. Thus, "officer, where's the injured party?"

2.23 Did You Take an Oath?

This question is asked, by nearly every sovereign citizen, and is asked repeatedly of the detaining officer. The sovereign citizen already knows the answer to the question, so it is not really a question at all. It is meant to be a reminder to the officer, of their oath and also an admonishment. The question is often asked, angrily and with growing anger every time it is asked. Remember, the sovereign citizen knows that the police officer has taken an oath. It is not as if they do not know the answer. It is not as if they ask the police officer and the police officer responds "yes, I have" whereupon the sovereign citizen replies "wow, I didn't know you really took an oath. Thanks officer, good to know." That would be a friendly exchange and a legitimate question. No matter what the officer responds, the sovereign citizen will continue to "ask" the same question. "Officer, did you take an oath?" No answer, provided by the officer, will have any impact on this behavior by the sovereign citizen, except to make the sovereign citizen more frustrated and angry. It is important to focus on the anger of the sovereign citizen. This growing anger may only result in the sovereign citizen being impolite and rude to the police officer but the growing anger and frustration might also result in the death of the police officer. Sovereign citizens, have proven to be a great danger to police officers. Many sovereign citizens, believe that they have the right to kill police officers, when they deem it necessary, like when they are being "illegally" detained. Some sovereign citizens believe that they may kill police officers without fear of recrimination.

When the sovereign citizen asks "officer, have you taken an oath?" they are in reality shouting an admonishment at the police officer, not asking a question. The sovereign citizen believes that the police officer, because of the oath the officer has taken, can only provide for public safety. The sovereign citizen believes the police officer is only empowered to keep them safe. They are not empowered to enforce traffic laws or detain the sovereign citizen or most certainly not arrest the sovereign citizen.

Sovereign citizens would consider any activity by the police officer, other than providing for public safety, an illegal act. They refer to this as "acting under the color of law." In the minds of sovereign citizens, when a police officer performs an illegal act, under the "color of law," the sovereign citizen has the right to shoot and kill that police officer. Also remember, that sovereign citizens believe they are immune to gun laws. Many carry weapons without a concealed carry permit. They believe it is their constitutional right to do so. They believe they have a right to use those weapons to defend themselves against corrupt actions by police officers, acting under the color of law.

This is not to say that every sovereign citizen is armed or that every sovereign citizen, if so armed, would decide to shoot a police officer. However, some have done so and many more sincerely believe they have the right to do so. The incensed anger of the sovereign citizen combined with their righteous indignation, would surely result in the death of more police officers, if more sovereign citizens were armed or if armed sovereign citizens had sufficient courage.

2.24 What Crime Am I Being Accused of Committing?

The sovereign citizen believes that the police may only stop them, if they are being accused of having committed a criminal offense. When the sovereign citizen asks that question, they are asserting their assumption that a police officer does not have the right to stop them for a traffic violation. They are, in essence, arguing that the traffic stop is invalid. This argument often continues throughout the entirety of the traffic stop and becomes the basis for the sovereign citizen's failure to comply with the officer's commands. In the mind of the sovereign citizen, there is no need to comply with anything that the officer requests. No need to show the officer a driver's license, no need for the drivers to identify themselves, no need for the driver to show proof of insurance or vehicle registration, etc. Most importantly, since the traffic stop is invalid, the sovereign citizen does not need to exit the vehicle when told to do so or unlock their doors. This often results in the need for the police officer to break one or more windows of the sovereign citizens' vehicle, so as to gain access. When told by the police officer that they are under arrest and must exit the vehicle, the sovereign citizen will respond to the police officer by saying "no I am not under arrest." Often, the sovereign citizen, must be tased and physically dragged from their vehicle. The sovereign citizen does not go passively or willingly. Savage struggles have occurred, resulting in the death of the police officer or the sovereign citizen.

The nexus of the issues, is the belief by the sovereign citizen that police only have power over crimes and traffic offenses are not crimes. The sovereign citizen is wrong on both assumptions. Obviously, the individuals in uniform, sitting in boldly marked police cars, commonly known as police officers do have power over traffic offenses because thousands of police officers, make arrests at traffic stops every day.

Are traffic laws classified as crimes? Some are. Think of vehicular homicide, as an example. Some traffic laws are classified as being something other than "criminal." It makes absolutely no difference how they are classified. The police officer does have power at a traffic stop to enforce the law. There is no need to debate the power of the police officer at a traffic stop. Law enforcement at traffic stops, is practiced, every day, in every state, in every city, in every county, in every township, in every municipality, of the U.S. Sovereign citizens lose on this one. They do so every time, and often in a spectacular fashion that includes flying glass, screams and the enlightening experience of 10,000 volts of electricity, surging through one's body.

2.25 Am I Being Detained?

That is a question asked and asked endlessly, by the sovereign citizen at every traffic stop. Starting soon after the traffic stop, the sovereign citizen will begin to ask the officer "am I being detained?" The officer will reply "yes, you are being detained." The sovereign citizen then replies "am I free to leave?" The police officer will reply "no, you are being detained and are not free to leave." The sovereign citizen, will ask either "am I being detained?" or "am I free to leave?" through the entirety of the traffic stop. Being detained by a police officer, means by definition, one is not free to leave. That is what detention means. Once the police officer tells the sovereign citizen that they are not free to leave, then it automatically means that they are being detained. When the police officer tells the sovereign citizen that they are being detained, it automatically means that they are not free to leave. Yet, the sovereign citizen asks these questions, over and over again, often several times per minute.

Obviously, these are not legitimate questions by a sovereign citizen. When the words "am I free to leave?" or "am I being detained?" leave the mouth of the sovereign citizen, they were never meant to be a question. The sovereign citizen is never surprised by the answer of the police officer and once the police officer gives their answer, there is absolutely no need for the sovereign citizen to "ask" again. Yet, they do, over and over again, perhaps many dozens of times. Is the sovereign citizen, hard of hearing? Obviously, not. They clearly hear and respond to the police officer during the other parts of the traffic stop but they repeatedly ask the same questions, "am I free to leave? or "am I being detained?" No matter how many times the police officer answers the same question, the sovereign citizen will ask it again, as if it were never answered or as if the sovereign citizen is revealing a grand deficit in their short-term memory.

2.26 You Are Dismissed

The sovereign citizen, very literally believes that a police officer is a servant. To be more specific, they believe that the police officer is technically a public servant and since the sovereign citizen is a member of the public, the police officer is their servant. Servants have employers and follow the orders of their employers and are paid by their employers. In the mind of the sovereign citizen, the public pays the salary of the police officer and since the sovereign citizen is a member of the public, at least in part, it is the sovereign citizen who pays the salary of the police officer. The police officer is thus their servant and when stopped by a police officer, they need to say no more than "you are dismissed." In practice, the sovereign citizen will say exactly those words to the police officer, over and over again. The sovereign citizen will perhaps talk to the police officer politely at first but as their frustration grows, they then begin to shout and use obscenities.

It does not occur to the sovereign citizen that the police officer serves the public at large and not any one individual. Of course, it borders on insanity to believe that a police officer is there to serve you and when you are displeased with the police officer, you may simply wave your hand and say "you are dismissed." The police officer serves the public by enforcing the laws that were created by the public. Police officers enforce laws. They never create laws. They never interpret law. Legislatures, create laws. Judges, interpret laws. Police officers enforce laws. They serve and protect the public by arresting those who break the law. They are not personal servants of sovereign citizens and respond not at all to the words "you are dismissed."

2.27 Lie to Police

The most obvious example, of sovereign citizens lying to police officers, is their claiming that their vehicle windows are broken and can only be rolled down an inch or two. When asked by the officer to roll down their window, they will state that their window does not roll down any further or less frequently, they will roll it down another inch and then say "that's as far as it goes, my window is broken." The police officer will often say that they cannot hear the sovereign citizen and carrying on a conversation, in this manner, is not safe. The sovereign citizen will often say "I can hear you just fine." Sometimes the sovereign citizen simply refuses to roll the window down any further stating that they are more comfortable with the window being cracked only an inch or two. Under these circumstances, the police officers will turn their head to the side in an attempt to hear what the sovereign citizen is saying and in doing so turns their eyes away from the sovereign citizen. Forcing the police officer to turn his eyes away from the sovereign citizen, most certainly puts the police officer in greater danger.

The sovereign citizen seems to have no hesitation in lying to the police officer. Some will claim to personally know their chief of police, who has already personally reassured them that they do not need a driver's license or to register their vehicles. They may lie to the police officer and suggest that the officer is wasting their time as the sovereign citizen has gone to court multiple times in the last few months and in every case the judge has ruled in their favor. They will lie about their address. They will lie about their name. They will claim to have no working phone number. They will claim that they do not know their own name. They will claim that they do not have a name, only an appellation (title). They will tell the police officer that they cannot tell the officer their name because they do not want to lie to the officer. They do not know what their real name is, only the name that people have called them or the name taught to them by their parents. Since the sovereign citizen has no way to verify the accuracy of that name, they will not provide it to the police officer so as not to be guilty of deception or lying.

Their tactics of lies and deceptions, never seem to go well for the sovereign citizen. After a lengthy interaction, lasting as long as an hour, the sovereign citizen often has both driver's and passenger's windows smashed. This is often followed, by pepper spray, tasing, violent removal from the vehicle and subsequent arrest.

2.28 I Demand to Speak to Your Supervisor

A traffic stop of a sovereign citizen can easily take up to one hour, require three or four police vehicles and sometimes more. The traffic citation given to a sovereign citizen is a very costly expense to society at large. When three or four police vehicles, each containing two officers, are assigned to a traffic stop for up to one hour's time, the cost to society is high. Multiple police vehicles, need not be assigned to the ordinary traffic stop. A non-sovereign citizen traffic stop may only require one officer and average 15 minutes or less. Extra officers are assigned to these traffic stops because of the fear of violence from the sovereign citizen and their refusal to cooperate.

In most cases, the sovereign citizen will demand that they no longer speak to any officer on site and will speak only to their supervisor. Part of the lengthy delay, is due to the time necessary for the supervisor to arrive at the traffic stop. There is an old saying "time is money." When it comes to police officers, that saying could be modified to "time is safety." The more officers at a traffic stop, the fewer that are available to tend to public safety. The longer a traffic stop takes, the less time there is to stop other speeders and violators of the law. Make no mistake, the existence and availability of police services is exactly what allows a society to function in relative safety. The less police services, the less safe is every member of our society. Available police services should not be squandered or wasted on the frivolous antics of sovereign citizens.

Chapter 3
Violence and Sovereign Citizens

Despite the fact that there is very little empirical research about sovereign citizens, a narrative has developed that they rarely engage in violence. Perhaps this is because of their well-known association with committing acts of paper terrorism, a term that refers to the use of legal loopholes to attempt to circumvent the law (Southern Poverty Law Center 2017). Chapter three challenges the view that sovereign citizens are seldom violent by exploring acts of violence committed by sovereign citizens in furtherance of their anti-government agenda.

For reasons that are not entirely evident, a narrative has emerged that characterizes sovereign citizens as being rarely involved in violence. While they are better known for committing paper terrorism, they have undoubtably committed a considerable number of violent acts. Lest we forget that the deadliest domestic terrorism incident in U.S. history was in part, carried out by Terry Nichols, an accomplice of Timothy McVeigh, and a self-described sovereign citizen (Challacombe and Lucas 2019).

One congressman in particular seems to appreciate the risk posed by sovereign citizens. Beginning as early as 2012, U.S. Representative Cedric Richmond of Louisiana was calling for an increased focus on sovereign citizens (Report on Legislative and Oversight Activities 2012). In October 2012, he sent a letter to the Homeland Security committee chairman asking to expand the scope of the hearings to cover domestic extremism (Report on Legislative and Oversight Activities 2012). In subsequent hearings, Rep. Richmond continued to reiterate his concerns. In a September 2016 House of Representatives Committee on Homeland Security meeting, Rep. Richmond again tried to warn the committee about the dangers of sovereign citizens. "They shot down three officers in Baton Rouge, injured another couple… sovereign citizens have killed more police officers than anybody else" (Stopping the Next Attack 2016). The case he is referring is that of Gavin Long. Mr.

The original version of this chapter was revised. The correction to this chapter is available at https://doi.org/10.1007/978-3-030-45851-5_8

© The Author(s), under exclusive license to Springer Nature Switzerland AG 2020, Corrected Publication 2020
C. M. Sarteschi, *Sovereign Citizens*, SpringerBriefs in Psychology, https://doi.org/10.1007/978-3-030-45851-5_3

Long shot six police officers, three of whom died from their wounds. Mr. Long claimed to be a member of the United Washitaw de Dugdahmoundyah Muur Nation, a well-known sovereign citizen group who believes their ancient Moroccan heritage makes them exempt from U.S. laws (Hilleary 2016). The threat posed to law enforcement and society at large, by sovereign citizens, is real.

As with any understudied phenomenon, it is important to explore the full scope of the movement. In an effort to understand the nature of sovereign citizen violence, 214 cases of sovereign citizen violence or planned acts of violence, between 1990 and 2019, were collected. An individual is considered a sovereign citizen if they have self-identified as such or when their core beliefs are consistent with that of sovereign citizens (see chapter two for more on their core beliefs). Cases included in the database where both those charged with the following crimes and those were the sovereign citizen had threatened or plotted to engage in one or more of the following crimes: murder, rape, sexual assault, robbery, aggravated assault, simple assault, and child pornography. Sources for data collection included: Google alerts, the Anti-Defamation League (ADL), social media sites such as Twitter, Reddit, and YouTube, journal articles, the Southern Poverty Law Center (SPLC), the Global Terrorism Database (GTD) via the University of Maryland, the blog kept by Daryl Johnson, former U.S. federal intelligence analyst for the Department of Homeland Security, the personal website of J.J. McNabb, who tracks cases of extremism, and The Center for Investigative Reporting.

It should be noted that not all cases were easily categorizable. Part of the challenge involves the fact that there are no clear-cut definitions on what constitutes a sovereign citizen. There is no official governmental "authority" on sovereign citizens or even an agreed upon definition. In addition, some sovereign citizens subscribe to a number of belief systems that span multiple categories. For instance, Jerad and Amanda Miller are considered sovereign citizens in this data collection effort; however, they could also be categorized as belonging to the patriot or militia movement.

3.1 Andrew Joseph Stack

Much like Jerad and Amanda Miller, Andrew Joseph Stack is another case that is not easy to categorize. Mr. Stack flew his plane into an IRS building in Austin, Texas (Graham 2010). He expressed an extreme displeasure with the government and in particular the IRS. He discussed the "sovereignty" of "individuals and their right to withhold taxes" (Flowers 2018). Though he seemed to espouse beliefs consistent with the sovereign citizens movement, and has been characterized as such by a number of sources (e.g. Sherrow 2012), he could also be categorized as a member of the tax protester group which many feel may have been a precursor to the sovereign citizen movement. In many cases, there are obvious overlaps between sovereign citizens and the broader patriot/alt-right/American far-right movement in general but such discussions are beyond the scope of this chapter. The following narrative describes some of the more notable cases of sovereign citizen violence.

3.2 Jerry Kane Jr. and Joseph Kane

One of the most documented and notorious cases of extreme sovereign citizen violence is the killing of two West Memphis, Arkansas law enforcement officers at the hands of Jerry Kane Jr. and his son Joseph. On the morning of May 20, 2010, officers Brandon Paudert and Bill Evans pulled over a white minivan with unusual license plates. The driver of the van, Jerry Kane Jr. claimed to be a pastor of an Ohio church (Paudert 2017). He proceeded to give the officers the typical pseudolegal paperwork, presented during traffic stops by sovereign citizens, including a homemade "travelers" card (Paudert 2017). According to reports, the officers were peacefully speaking to Mr. Kane, near the back of the vehicle, when his 16-year-old son Joseph emerged with an assault rifle and began shooting (Dewan and Hubbell, 2010). Officer Paudert was shot 11 times and officer Evans was shot 14 times. Both officers died from their wounds. After shooting the officers, the Kanes fled the scene. Approximately 90 minutes later, the police caught up with them. Both suspects exchanged gunfire with police. They wounded two additional police officers before being killed, themselves (Dewan and Hubbell 2010).

One of the two officers killed by the Kanes, was officer Brandon Paudert, the son of Bob Paudert, also a law enforcement officer. Interviewed by *The Washington Post*, he recalled the time when he learned his son had been killed by two sovereign citizens. "I found him with the back of his head shot off. It was a horrible, horrible scene. I didn't care about going to work after that. I lost my passion for law enforcement that day" (Holley 2017). When investigating his son's case, he learned that the FBI had known about the Kanes but had not shared that information with local law enforcement (Paudert 2017). At the time of the incident, Bob Paudert indicated that "not one chief or sheriff I spoke to afterward knew about sovereign citizens." He now travels the country warning those in law enforcement about the dangers of sovereign citizens.

3.3 Nathaniel "Sach" Kargas

In another case involving a father-son pair of sovereign citizens, two Alaskan troopers Sgt. Patrick "Scott" Johnson and Gabriel "Gabe" Rich were shot and killed by 21-year-old Nathaniel "Sach" Kargas. The shooting occurred after Nathaniel's father Arvin threatened to shoot an unarmed peace officer. He argued with the officer, claiming that he had no jurisdiction to arrest him (Gettys 2014). Realizing the need for armed back up, the peace officer called the troopers who flew in to arrest Arvin on a misdemeanor assault charge and suspended license (Gettys 2014). Arvin resisted arrest and fought with the troopers. During the struggle, the three men fell to the floor and into the house. Attempting to protect his father, Nathaniel went into his parents' bedroom, loaded an assault rifle and shot the troopers. Seven bullets were fired; five hit the troopers, none hit his father. Reports indicated that Nathaniel shot the gun with accuracy and precision, as he carefully managed not to shoot his father who was wrestling underneath the troopers. Nathaniel received a mandatory 99-year prison sentence for each murder. Arvin Kangas received an eight-year sentence for manipulating the trooper's bodies and guns to make it appear as though they had drawn their weapons during their arrest attempt (Associated Press 2016b).

After the shooting, it was revealed that Arvin was part of a small group of troublemakers in the village who called themselves the "Athabascan nation" (Cole 2016). They were known for their hatred of law enforcement, argued for the need for Alaskan natives to take back traditional territory, and rejected the jurisdiction of public officials (Shedlock 2014). They regularly threatened tribal staff with deadly weapons who, on at least five occasions, were forced to close their offices (Shedlock 2014). After the trials of both father and son, the Tanana Tribal Council voted to banish Arvin and one other man from the village because "these individuals continue to present a danger to the peace, morals, culture and physical and general welfare of the community" (Shedlock 2014, para 11). Prior to the shootings, Nathaniel was known as kindhearted and well-mannered. His father, on the other hand, was alleged to have been abusive towards his family and was considered a radical for his beliefs. Many blamed Arvin for radicalizing his son Nathaniel with his "uncensored and dangerous" sovereign citizen views (Shedlock 2014).

3.4 Jered and Amanda Miller

On June 8, 2014, two Las Vegas Metropolitan police officers Igor Soldo and Alyn Beck were eating lunch at a local pizzeria. Unbeknownst to them, they were being stalked by a sovereign citizen couple named Jered and Amanda Miller who had been plotting to kill law enforcement officers in hopes of sparking a revolt against the government. After choosing their targets in the restaurant, the couple simultaneously began shooting. Both officers were shot and fatally wounded. As their bodies lay on the ground, the Millers stole their weapons and ammunition. They then draped one of the officer's bodies with a Gadsden flag (a yellow banner with a picture of a coiled rattlesnake, that reads "Don't Tread on Me"), the other with a swastika pin and a handwritten note that read "This is the start of the revolution" signed by both husband and wife (MacNab 2014). Killing the officers took only four seconds.

Heavily armed, the couple fled to a nearby Walmart. Once inside, Jerad retrieved a cart and began shouting about the revolution. He ordered customers to leave the store and shot one round into the ceiling. An armed customer named Joseph Wilcox decided to take action. As he approached Jerad, Amanda shot and killed Mr. Wilcox. Amanda was then shot by police in the right shoulder but was not fatally wounded. She then tried to shoot Jerad but he had already been shot by police. Soon thereafter, she shot herself in the right side of her head, an act of suicide. The Walmart incident lasted 24 minutes. Five people were killed that day. The couple's attack on law enforcement became the focus of an FBI documentary entitled *A Revolutionary Act* (Crosby 2019). It is now used to train both local and federal investigators about the dangers of violent extremists (Crosby 2019).

3.5 Stephen Paddock

Stephen Paddock, also known as the "Las Vegas shooter," killed 58 people and wounded nearly 900 more on October 1, 2017 in what authorities have described as the "largest mass casualty shooting in this country's history" (LVMPD criminal investigative report 2018, p. 125). Investigations did not uncover a motive for Paddock's actions. Though no definitive motive was identified, he did express ideas consistent with sovereign citizen ideology. Days before the shooting, for instance, a witness overheard him discussing courtroom flags with gold fringes as not being real flags (Wilson 2018). The claim that gold fringed flags are really "admiralty flags" (and thus the cases should be heard by an admiralty court) is a common claim espoused by sovereign citizens. That same witness also heard him discussing the 25th anniversary of the Ruby Ridge standoff and the Waco siege (Wilson 2018). Other witnesses recounted Mr. Paddock discussing Federal Emergency Management Agency (FEMA) camps and other "antigovernment" ideas. The FEMA camp conspiracy theory holds that the purpose of the agency is to build concentration camps to house "patriots" after the government declares martial law as part of their "New World Order" plan (Wilson 2018). These ideas can be traced back to the Posse Comitatus movement, from which the sovereign citizen movement is said to have derived (Wilson 2018). Though it is impossible to know with certainty whether Steven Paddock was a full-fledged sovereign citizen, he did express ideas consistent with the sovereign citizen movement.

3.6 Travis Reinking

Another self-identified sovereign citizen mass shooter is Travis Reinking. Mr. Reinking shot and killed four people and injured several others during a mass shooting at a waffle house in Tennessee (Perez 2018). According to police reports, Mr. Reinking referred to himself as a sovereign citizen after a July 2017 arrest in reference to his attempting to visit Donald Trump to declare his sovereignty and inspect the grounds of the White House (Bidgood 2018; Montgomery 2018).

3.7 Jared Loughner

Jared Loughner pled guilty to 19 charges of murder and attempted murder, after a Tucson Arizona shooting on January 8, 2011. Six people were killed and 14 others were injured, including U.S. Representative Gabrielle Giffords who was shot in the head and survived. Mr. Loughner was known to have been preoccupied with theories of government fraud. He often made statements about "grammar," "the ratifications" and the "new currency" (Sharrock 2011). A well-known "guru" of the sovereign citizen movement, David Wynn Miller, told *The New York Times* that Mr.

Loughner had "probably been on my website" (Sharrock 2011). Mr. Miller explicitly focused on grammar as being important. He taught his followers that any word in the English language that starts with a vowel, followed by two consonants, "is a word that means no contract" (Netolitzky 2018, p. 1062). *Mother Jones* magazine identified a number of additional statements Mr. Loughner made in YouTube videos that strongly suggested his being a sovereign citizen. These included the following: "the government is implying my control and brainwash on the people by controlling grammar"; "I can't trust the current government because of ramifications"; "you don't have to accept the Federalist laws. Nonetheless, read the United States of America's Constitution to apprehend all of the current treasonous laws"; and "no, I won't pay debt with the currency that's not backed by gold and silver!" (Sharrock 2011).

3.8 Terry Lyn Smith

Terry Lyn Smith is a sovereign citizen and the patriarch of a seven-member group, many of whom are also considered sovereign citizens. Mr. Smith was charged with first-degree murder for shooting St. John the Baptist Sheriff's deputies, killing two and seriously injuring others (Galoaro 2012). He is currently serving a life sentence for rape in an unrelated case (Associated Press 2020). The incident occurred after one of the members of the group shot an off-duty deputy, and then fled to a nearby mobile home park in LaPlace, Louisiana where the subsequent ambush attack on officers occurred (Morlin 2018). In February 2020, his son, Kyle Joekel, was found guilty of first-degree murder for killing the deputies. At the time of this writing, a sentence had not yet been imposed (Associated Press 2020).

3.9 John Terry Chapman Jr

In another violent incident involving a sovereign citizen, John Terry Chapman Jr. was found guilty of shooting and wounding a Tulsa police officer at a local gas station on July 3, 2018. Bodycam footage shows that Mr. Chapman had been driving a vehicle without a valid driver's license and with a license plate registered to a different vehicle. During a traffic stop, officers explained his offenses and requested identification. Mr. Chapman refused to show identification, was uncooperative and argumentative. He repeatedly challenged the jurisdiction of the officers and requested that they call their supervisors, two common sovereign citizen tactics. When Mr. Chapman refused to leave his vehicle and continued to resist arrest, the sergeant who had arrived on scene to assist, deployed his PepperBall into the vehicle. Mr. Chapman responded by shooting the sergeant. The sergeant survived, thanks to a coin in his pocket that deflected the bullet (United States Department of Justice 2019).

3.10 Forrest Gordon Clark

Forrest Gordon Clark is a sovereign citizen and a neighborhood nuisance. He was known for being overtly religious, aggressive and moody (Cosgrove et al. 2018). In a recent incident, he is accused of setting the 2018 Holy Fire that burned 23,000 acres in California (California News Wire Service 2018). Tens of thousands of residents were forced to flee their homes. Officials consider it one of the "most destructive forest fires of 2018" (Thomas 2018).

In addition to arson charges, Mr. Clark has also been accused of resisting arrest and threatening to kill a neighbor ("Mark my words, you're going to die… I have 100 percent plausible deniability. You're going to die. I'm going to murder you") (City News Service 2018). When questioned by police about the fire, he blamed his neighbor after having allegedly learned about it in a "lucid dream." In subsequent versions, he blamed another neighbor and the "Mexicans" (California News Wire Service 2018).

J.J. MacNab reviewed eight years of Mr. Clark's social media posts and found, among many other conspiratorially-laden ideas, extensive evidence of his link to the sovereign citizen movement (Thomas 2018). For instance, he was active in the Restore America Plan which eventually became the Republic for the United States of America (RuSA). RuSA argues that the real US government has not existed since 1871 and has since been replaced with an imposter or shadow government. According to their website, RuSA has created its own parallel government that operates "along side" (sic) the "current corporate government system." She also found messages on his Facebook page in which he declares himself a "Sovereign Man," a "Kansas free state-interim representative" and a "DeJure grand Juror." He has plead not guilty.

3.11 Scott Roeder

Court records indicate that on May 31, 2009, Scott Roeder, anti-abortionist and sovereign citizen, shot Dr. George Tiller at point-blank range in the forehead during church services (*State of Kansas v. Roeder* 2014). Mr. Roeder quickly left the premises, was soon caught and confessed to the authorities. Mr. Roeder was a member of the "Montana Freemen," a group who has attempted to establish their own government and financial system. They were known for holding seminars in which they taught adherents about running financial scams. They operated out of a rural schoolhouse in Montana on property they referred to as "Justus Township." Though many of their crimes were financial in nature, the FBI considers them capable of violence in part because their members are often heavily armed. The group embarked upon an 81-day standoff with the FBI in 1996 when a local bank foreclosed on their leader's property (Montana Freemen standoff 2016). Several group members threatened extreme violence against judges and other public officials in letters, indicating that "Our special Orders…is for our special appointed Constables and our Lawful

Posse to shoot to kill any public hireling [sic] and fourteenth amendment citizen who in caught in any act whatsoever on taking private property" (United States v. John P. McGuire United States of America v. Cherlyn Petersen 2002, para. 4).

During a traffic stop in 1996, Mr. Roeder had a homemade license plate that read "Sovereign Citizen." He had no driver's license or vehicle registration or insurance. In his car, the police found explosive charges, a fuse cord, a pound of gun powder, and nine-volt batteries. He subsequently served 24 months of probation. While on probation, he failed to pay his taxes or give his employer his social security number. He appealed his case involving the car search and it was overturned (Doctor's alleged killer had 'sovereign' ties 2009). In a 50-minute video interview with Mr. Roeder from 1996, that aired on a public access cable show in 2010, he discussed his belief that he has a "God-given right to travel" without a driver's license (Hegeman 2010). He believes that "under God's law you are free to do anything that does not break God's law and does not harm anyone else" (Hegeman 2010). Mr. Roeder is eligible for parole after serving 25 years for the murder of Dr. Tiller ("Man who killed late-term abortion doctor" 2016).

3.12 Attempts, Threats, Unsuccessful Plots, and Jailhouse Conversions

A Massachusetts man identified as posting information consistent with sovereign citizen ideology threatened to kill police after he was charged with driving an unregistered and uninsured motor vehicle. Shortly after the incident he sent the police private messages indicating that "I will travel freely upon any public road in any public highway I please until the day I die. This is my notice to your department. I will call 911 on any officer that illegally tries to pull me over and or detains me without probable cause while I am using my automobile in a safe manner." In another private message to police, he wrote: "I have the right to kill a cop who violates my constitutional rights when I am exercising them" (LaBella 2018, para 24). Media reports indicated that the man had an extensive and violent criminal history.

3.13 Janay Rebecca Smith

Another case involves Pennsylvania Moorish sovereign citizen Janay Rebecca Smith (AKA Jahnay Rebekkah Bey). She was pulled over by police after failing to stop at multiple signs. After the officer approached the vehicle, she refused to roll down her window more than a few inches, and would only provide a self-created identification card referring to herself as an "American National." When the police could find no record of a driver's license for her, they detained her and she subsequently began to resist and refused to exit the car. The officers attempted to forcibly remove her and as she struggled, she put the car in drive and drove away dragging one officer 10 to 15 feet. The police eventually caught up with her about 30 minutes later and she was arrested (Rellahan 2019). Court records indicate that she is facing both felony and misdemeanor charges for the incident.

3.14 Mitchell Timothy Taebel

Officers attempted to pull over Mitchell Timothy Taebel, a self-identified sovereign citizen, speeding through downtown Phoenix, Arizona. When he refused to stop, a police chase ensued. When the suspect was stopped at a red light, officers attempted to box him in but he rammed one of their vehicles and sped away, weaving in and out of traffic on the highway. During the high-speed chase, the suspect called 911 to report that the police had "no probable cause." The chase came to an end after the suspect wrecked his vehicle, slamming head on into another vehicle and injuring two people. During his arraignment, he brazenly told the court that "officers can be killed under USC section 241 and 242. I just want to put that on record, and should be, in my opinion." He then subsequently held a press conference in which he made similar claims about his belief that he has the right to kill law enforcement officers and threatened to sue all of the public officials involved in his case.

Another sovereign citizen stated in no uncertain terms that he has the right to kill an officer during an incident in August 2019. Press accounts indicate that a sovereign citizen was experiencing a medical problem inside a McDonald's restaurant. The police were called and upon arrival, they learned that the sovereign citizen had an active warrant for trespassing and placed him under arrest. The officers began searching his backpack and he became upset. It was at this point that he identified himself as a "sovereign citizen" and declared that he had "every right to kill" the officer. The sovereign citizen then became agitated, combative, and, in a struggle, reached for the officer's firearm. He succeeded, pulling the trigger causing the gun to discharge. The bullet struck the officer's cell phone and his thigh causing a laceration around four inches long. It was later learned that the suspect's backpack contained a full syringe of methamphetamine, and a marijuana smoking device (Adams 2019).

In April 2016, two Ohio sovereign citizens were arrested after accidentally exploding a homemade bomb they planned to use to rob a bank or an armored car (Associated Press 2016a). One of the men lost both of his hands in the explosion. The main suspect was sentenced to 14 years in prison.

3.15 Michael Wayne Parsons

A trio of sovereign citizens, Michael Wayne Parsons, his wife Patricia Parsons, and Suzanne Holland, (a Canadian also known as Zsuzsanna Hegedus), are alleged to have plotted to kidnap a Nebraska sheriff and a Tennessee judge in 2017 (Bolan

2017). It all began after Mr. Parsons removed his ankle monitor and was attempting to flee the country. He had been scheduled to appear in state court on two counts of being a felon in possession of a firearm.

When he failed to appear in court, a warrant was issued. Mr. Parsons was subsequently located by authorities at an airfield in Nebraska, after having grounded his single engine airplane. Mr. Parsons was in possession of several hundred rounds of ammunition and an assault rifle.

Once Mr. Parsons was taken into custody, Mrs. Parsons and Ms. Holland (self-appointed chief justice of the Universal Supreme Court in Canada), sent fake legal paperwork to the jail and issued orders that Mr. Parsons be released (Bolan 2017). When those were ignored, they tried issuing "warrants" demanding the arrest and extradition of the sheriff and the Tennessee judge. To assist in their efforts, they contacted a New Orleans bounty hunter who, unbeknownst to them, turned out to be an FBI confidential informant. They agreed to pay the "bounty hunter" $250,000 to break Mr. Parsons out of jail, and to transport the sheriff and the judge to Canada "to answer charges" supposedly brought against them by the universal court (United States Department of Justice 2017). They agreed upon an initial payment of $5000 for travel arrangements and to pay 30 operatives to carry out the plan (Maxey 2017). When they could not acquire the money for the initial payment, the women asked their source to accept a Corvette instead but ended up providing a 1991 Ford Ranger pickup as a down payment, in place of the Corvette (Maxey 2017). Mrs. Parsons was arrested before the plot was carried out and eventually pleaded guilty to aiding and abetting solicitation to commit kidnapping (United States Department of Justice 2017). It is unclear whether Suzanne Holland has ever faced punishment by the Canadian authorities for her role in the plot (Johnson 2018).

Mr. Parsons had a history of problems with the law. He has been previously convicted of drinking while intoxicated (DWI), and aggravated assault after holding two neighbors at gunpoint during an "citizen's arrest." (Johnson 2018). In court, he causes problems by using a variety of delay tactics. These include his claim of diplomatic immunity from prosecution because he is the Associate Chief Justice and Ambassador of the Tsilhqot'in nation, country of Chilcotin; claiming the court has no jurisdiction over him because it lists his name in all capital letters, which, in his view, indicates a corporation rather than the "life man"; filing documents with nonsensical claims titled "Special Appearance Only" or a "Notice" to transfer jurisdiction "in all cases Affecting Ambassadors for a New Trial or ORDER an Acquittal," refusing court-appointed lawyers and instead choosing to represent himself (*State of Tennessee v. Parsons* 2018). These frivolous notions, put forth by Mr. Parsons, have all failed in the courtroom.

3.16 Ted Klaudt

In 2008, former South Dakota Republican state representative Ted Klaudt was convicted of four counts of second-degree rape. The victims were his two foster daughters. Court records indicate Mr. Klaudt devised an elaborate scheme in which he would trick his underage foster daughters into allowing him to perform lengthy and sometimes painful gynecological exams on them in hotel rooms. The purpose of the exams, he claimed, was assisting them in donating their reproductive eggs to couples for payment. As part of the ploy to convince the girls to allow him to inspect their bodies, he created the fake persona of "Terri Linee" who he alleged was an agent for the egg donation agency. "Terri" would send emails to the girls encouraging exams in exchange for payment and threatened them if they refused. The court recognized the crimes of Mr. Klaudt as being overwhelmingly psychologically damaging to the girls. He took advantage of young and vulnerable girls, with troubled histories, who trusted and respected their foster father and state representative. Evidence of psychological coercion, the court noted, was substantial. Mr. Klaudt was sentenced to 44 years for the rape charges and an additional 10 years for tampering with evidence (Ellis 2017).

Since his conviction, Mr. Klaudt has attempted to utilize a number of common sovereign citizen tactics from prison. In 2009, he sent a "common law copyright notice" to news outlets warning them against using his name without his consent. He claims that no one is allowed to use his name without his consent and anyone who does so owes him $500,000 (Brokaw 2009). Jonathan Ellis of the *Argus Leader* (2017) reported that in 2010, Mr. Klaudt sent a letter to President Obama renouncing his citizenship and claimed that his trial was an unlawful military tribunal. He wrote letters to a federal judge claiming that he had evidence that the state had misused federal funds and threatened to turn over those documents to *Fox News* if these legal problems were not resolved. In 2018, the court outlined a number of civil claims he argued pro se, including that he has "only given up [his] U.S. citizenship NOT [his] American citizenship" and his belief that there are "two sources of citizenship, and only two: birth [in the United States] and naturalization." Based on his "extensive amount of research" he has "come to realize that the US is nothing more than a Corporation…which has been re-incorporated several times over." These and other sovereign citizen arguments, based on the idea of "corporate citizenship," were deemed "nonsensical" by the court and dismissed (*Klaudt v. State of South Dakota* et al. 2018, para. 2).

3.17 Steven Lorenzo

Steven Lorenzo is a serial rapist, convicted of drugging, raping and sexually torturing nine gay men. He is also one of the most notorious figures in Tampa Bay, Florida history. In 2017, he was charged with murder involving two cases more than a decade old. In court, he declared himself a "sovereign man." He refused to enter a plea, chose to represent himself, as many sovereign citizens do, and claimed that the court has no jurisdiction over him (Sullivan 2017). He told the court: "this is a fiction, corporate court; I am not a corporate person. I am a living, breathing being" (Sullivan 2017). His sovereign citizen defense was rejected.

3.18 The Insane Deuces

Two members of The Insane Deuces, a notorious and dangerous northern Illinois street gang, attempted to appeal their RICO conspiracy and murder charges by mounting a sovereign citizen defense. According to court records, in 2002 alone, the gang committed four murders, 11 attempted murders, two solicitations to commit murder, and were involved in multiple other shootings (United States Court of Appeals 2011). Both men were involved in an "ill-conceived campaign to obstruct the trial with repeated outbursts," by claiming the government had no jurisdiction over them and that they were "flesh and blood human beings." One filed more than 20 pro se documents referring to himself as a "sovereign secured party creditor," claiming to be "sovereign," immune from prosecution, demanding explanations for the gold fringe on the flag in the courtroom, and asserting that "no one can explain to me why the United States has to operate as a corporation" (*United States v. Benabe* 2011). Like many others before them, their sovereign citizen arguments were dismissed.

The aforementioned cases describe sovereign citizens who committed terrible acts of violence or who threatened to do so. Even in cases where a sovereign citizen may have also belonged to another extremist group, the common denominator among all of these individuals is their willingness to break the law and engage in violence. Sovereign citizens believe without evidence, and in the face of evidence to the contrary, that they have the right to do what they want. They make bold claims, are obstinate and are often unrelenting in their efforts. They consider themselves immune from U.S. laws and regularly challenge the legal systems in our country. These narratives serve as evidence of their danger to law enforcement, public officials and to society at large.

References

Adams, J. (2019, September 4). Officer's thigh, cell phone shot following arrest of 'combative' man in Cape Girardeau, MO. *KFVS12*. Retrieved from https://www.kfvs12.com/2019/09/04/officers-thigh-cell-phone-shot-following-arrest-combative-man-cape-girardeau-mo/

Associated Press. (2016a, April 16). 2 Ohio men indicted on weapons charges after bomb blows off hands of suspect. *Cleveland.com*. Retrieved from https://www.cleveland.com/nation/2016/04/2_ohio_men_face_weapons_charge.html

Associated Press. (2016b, May 16). Alaska man convicted of murder in death of two troopers. *Daily Herald*. Retrieved from https://www.dailyherald.com/article/20160516/news/305169792

Associated Press. (2020 February 7). Man convicted in 2012 deaths of 2 Louisiana deputies. Retrieved from https://www.katc.com/news/covering-louisiana/man-convicted-in-2012-deaths-of-2-louisiana-deputies

Bidgood, J. (2018 April 23). Nashville suspect once called himself a 'sovereign citizen.' Police say. What is that? *The New York Times*. Retrieved from https://www.nytimes.com/2018/04/23/us/sovereign-citizen.html

Bolan, K. (2017, September 7). Real scoop: B.C. woman linked to bizarre U.S. kidnapping plot. *Vancouver Sun*. Retrieved from https://vancouversun.com/news/staff-blogs/real-scoop-b-c-woman-linked-to-bizarre-u-s-kidnapping-plot

Brokaw, C. (2009, December 15). Rapist, former lawmaker Ted Klaudt claims name copyright. *The Associated Press*. Retrieved fromhttps://rapidcityjournal.com/news/rapist-former-lawmaker-ted-klaudt-claims-name-copyright/article_03881cae-e9a3-11de-848e-001cc4c002e0.html

California News Wire Services, News Partner. (2018, December 28). Holy fire suspect ordered to stand trial on arson charges. *Patch.com*. Retrieved from https://patch.com/california/lakeelsinore-wildomar/holy-fire-suspect-ordered-stand-trial-arson-charges

Challacombe, D. J., & Lucas, P. A. (2019). Postdicting violence with sovereign citizen actors: An exploratory test of the TRAP-18. *Journal of Threat Assessment and Management, 6*(1), 51–59. https://doi.org/10.1037/tam0000105.

City News Service. (2018, December 26). Judge drops two counts against Holy fire suspect Forrest Gordon Clark in ongoing hearing. *Desert Sun*. Retrieved from https://www.desertsun.com/story/news/crime_courts/2018/12/26/holy-fire-suspect-forrest-clark-due-court-preliminary-hearing/2414315002/

Cole, D. (2016, September 28). Defendant shot state troopers on impulse, without thought, defenses. *Anchorage Daily News*. Retrieved from https://www.adn.com/crime-justice/article/kangas-trial/2016/05/09/?returnUrl=https%3A%2F%2Fwww.adn.com%2Fcrime-justice%2Farticle%2Fkangas-trial%2F2016%2F05%2F09%2F&cancelUrl=https%3A%2F%2Fwww.adn.com%2Fcrime-justice%2Farticle%2Fkangas-trial%2F2016%2F05%2F09%2F&op=link

Cosgrove, J., Reyes-Velarde, & Tchekmedyian, A. (2018, August 13). 'It's all going to burn:' man accused of setting Holy fire was a well-known troublemaker, neighbor say. *The Los Angeles Times*. Retrieved from https://www.latimes.com/local/lanow/la-me-holy-fire-arson-suspect-20180812-story.html

Crosby, R. (2019 May 31). Sovereign citizen threat looms 5 years after Cicis pizza attack. *Las Vegas Review-Journal*. Retrieved from https://www.reviewjournal.com/crime/sovereign-citizen-threat-looms-5-years-after-cicis-pizza-attack-1676703/

Dewan, S., & Hubbell, J. (2010, May 23). Antigovernment rage for father and son in police shooting. *The New York Times*. Retrieved from https://www.nytimes.com/2010/05/24/us/24arkansas.html

Doctor's alleged killer had 'sovereign' ties. (2009). *Southern Poverty Law Center*. Retrieved from https://www.splcenter.org/fighting-hate/intelligence-report/2009/doctors-alleged-killer-had-sovereign-ties

Ellis, J. (2017, July 12). Court denies former lawmakers bid for freedom. *Argus Leader*. Retrieved from https://www.argusleader.com/story/news/2017/07/12/court-denies-former-lawmakers-bid-freedom/473284001/

Flowers, K. (2018). *Sovereign citizens: The evolving subculture*. Unpublished PowerPoint slides. Retrieved from https://files.nc.gov/ncdor/documents/files/flowers_-_sovereign_citizens.pdf.

Galoaro, C. (2012, August 18). 7 suspects in St. John deputy shootings are tied to violent antigovernment group. *The Times-Picayune*. Retrieved from https://www.nola.com/news/crime_police/article_51c1694b-1fe3-5504-a74c-8396efb78db2.html

Gettys, T. (2014). Sovereign citizen's teen son kills two 'Alaska State troopers.' *Raw Story*. Retrieved from https://www.rawstory.com/2014/05/sovereign-citizens-teen-son-kills-two-alaska-state-troopers-reality-tv-stars-in-sofa-dispute/

Graham, D. A. (2010, February 18). Joseph Stack and right-wing terror: Isolated incidents or worrying trend? *Newsweek*. Retrieved from https://www.newsweek.com/joseph-stack-and-right-wing-terror-isolated-incidents-or-worrying-trend-214822

Hegeman, R. (2010.). Anti-abortion activist to sell video of Roeder. *The Wichita Eagle*. Retrieved from https://www.kansas.com/news/local/crime/article1024727.html

Hilleary, C. (2016, July 19). Baton Rouge shooter was avowed 'sovercign citizen.' *Voice of America News*. Retrieved from https://www.voanews.com/usa/baton-rouge-shooter-was-avowed-sovereign-citizen

Holley, P. (2017 February 23). Domestic terrorists killed his son. He wants Trump to remember that America makes extremists, too. *The Washington Post*. Retrieved from https://www.washingtonpost.com/news/post-nation/wp/2017/02/23/domestic-terrorists-killed-his-son-he-wants-trump-to-remember-america-makes-extremists-too/

Johnson, D. (2018). Sovereign citizens plotted jailbreak, abduction of sheriff and judge. *Southern Poverty Law Center*. Retrieved from https://www.splcenter.org/hatewatch/2018/09/06/sovereign-citizens-plotted-jailbreak-abduction-sheriff-and-judge

Klaudt v. State of South Dakota et al. (2018). 18–850. *United States District Court for the District of Columbia*.

LaBella, M. (2018, March 2). Man charged with sending police threatening messages. *The Eagle-Tribune*. Retrieved from https://www.eagletribune.com/news/haverhill/man-charged-with-sending-police-threatening-messages/article_88230f1e-b319-5e96-8995-69d096dd21cf.html

LVMPD criminal investigative report of the 1 October mass casualty shooting. (2018). *Las Vegas Metropolitan Police Department*. Retrieved from http://thepinetree.net/new/wp-content/uploads/2018/08/1-October-FIT-Criminal-Investigative-Report-FINAL_080318.pdf.

MacNab, J. J. (2014, June 13). What Las Vegas police killings show about evolving sovereign. *Forbes*. Retrieved from https://www.forbes.com/sites/jjmacnab/2014/06/13/what-las-vegas-police-killings-show-about-evolving-sovereign-movement/#54c82fd32a28

Man who killed late-term abortion doctor gets lighter sentence. *CBS News*. (2016). Retrieved from https://www.cbsnews.com/news/scott-roeder-man-who-killed-george-tiller-late-term-abortion-doctor-gets-new-lenient-sentence/

Maxey, R. (2017, December 13). Brighton woman gets 5-year sentence for elaborate kidnapping plot against judge, sheriff. *Commercial Appeal*. Retrieved from https://www.commercialappeal.com/story/news/2017/12/13/west-tennessee-woman-gets-60-month-sentence-bizarre-kidnapping-plot-against-judge-sheriff/948218001/

Montana Freemen standoff. (2016, January 12). Billings Gazette. Retrieved from https://billingsgazette.com/news/state-and-regional/montana/montana-freemen-standoff/collection_df534ac6-ada1-54ff-affa-2313a7baecc6.html#1

Montgomery, S. J. (2018, April 23). Waffle house shooting suspect called himself 'sovereign citizen' in 2017 white house arrest (update). *Complex Media Inc*. Retrieved from https://www.complex.com/life/2018/04/waffle-house-shooting-suspect-sovereign-citizen-2017-white-house-arrest

Morlin, B. (2018, March 27). Sovereign citizen murder trial set for October. *Southern Poverty Law Center*. Retrieved from https://www.splcenter.org/hatewatch/2018/03/27/sovereign-citizen-murder-trial-set-october

Netolitzky, D. (2018). Organized pseudolegal commercial arguments ["OPCA"] as magic in eremony. *Alberta Law Review, 55*(4). https://doi.org/10.29173/alr2485.

Southern Poverty Law Center. Paper terrorism. (2017). *Southern Poverty Law Center*. Retrieved from https://www.splcenter.org/fighting-hate/intelligence-report/2017/paper-terrorism

Paudert, B. (2017, February 15). My son was murdered in the line of duty by right-wing xtremist. Trump should focus on the threat posed by 'sovereign citizens' as told to Alex Paudert. *The Trace*. Received from https://www.thetrace.org/2017/02/right-wing-extremists-sovereign-citizens-target-law-enforcement-trump/

Perez, M. (2018 April 24). Waffle house shooting suspect Travis Reinking's $2 million bond revoked, judge orders. *Newsweek*. Retrieved from https://www.newsweek.com/travis-reinking-waffle-house-shooting-tennessee-bond-revoked-899576

Rellahan, M. P. (2019, February 18). Bill dropped for Immaculata student accused of dragging cop with car. *Daily Local News*. Retrieved from https://www.dailylocal.com/news/bail-dropped-for-immaculata-student-accused-of-dragging-cop-with/article_6a7451ce-32d9-11e9-99aa-e7964e185a78.html?utm_medium=social&utm_source=twitter&utm_campaign=user-share

Report on Legislative and Oversight Activities of the House Committee on Homeland Security Together with Additional Views, House of Representatives. (2012). 112th Cong. 533.

Sharrock, J. (2011). Explained: Jared Loughner's Grammar Obsession. *Mother Jones*. Retrieved from https://www.motherjones.com/politics/2011/01/sovereign-citizens-jared-lee-loughner/

Shedlock, J, (2014). Tanana man sues village council for banishing him over 'radical' beliefs, alleged threats. *Anchorage Daily News*. Retrieved from https://www.adn.com/crime-justice/article/tanana-resident-sues-village-illegal-banishment-sentencing/2014/08/27/

References

Sherrow, V. (2012). *Homegrown Terror: The Oklahoma City Bombing*. New York: Enslow Publishers.

State of Kansas v. Roeder, (2014). 104, 520. *Supreme Court of the State of Kansas*.

State of Tennessee v. Parsons, (2018). W2018–00144-CCA-R3-CD. *Court of Criminal Appeals of Tennessee*.

Stopping the Next Attack: How to Keep Our City Streets from Becoming the Battleground. (2016). *Hearing Before Committee on Homeland Security, House of Representatives*, 114th Cong. 44. (testimony of Sheriff Jerry L. Demings).

Sullivan, D. (2017, December 4). Steve Lorenzo says double jeopardy trumps Tampa murder case. Is he right? *Tampa Bay Times*. Retrieved from https://www.tampabay.com/news/courts/criminal/Steven-Lorenzo-says-double-jeopardy-trumps-Tampa-murder-case-Is-he-right-_163273943

Thomas, J. L. (2018, August 13). Man accused of igniting CA wildfire is sovereign citizen with possible KS connection. *The Kansas City Star*. Retrieved from https://www.kansascity.com/news/state/kansas/article216582525.html

United States Department of Justice. (2017 September 1). *Tennessee woman pleads guilty to aiding and abetting an attempt to kidnap judge and sheriff in one-count criminal information*. [Press release]. Retrieved from https://www.justice.gov/usao-wdtn/pr/tennessee-woman-pleads-guilty-aiding-and-abetting-attempt-kidnap-judge-and-sheriff-one

United States Department of Justice. (2019 January 29). *Jury convicts Tulsa man of shooting a police officer*. [Press release]. Retrieved from https://www.justice.gov/usao-ndok/pr/jury-convicts-tulsa-man-shooting-police-officer

United States v. Benabe. (2011). 654 F.3d 753. *Court of Appeals for the Seventh Circuit*.

United States v. John P. McGuire United States of America v. Cherlyn Peterson. (2002). 307 F.3d. 1192. *ourt of Appeals for the Ninth Circuit*.

Wilson, J. (2018, May 19). New documents suggest Las Vegas shooter was conspiracy theorist – hat we know. *The Guardian*. Retrieved from https://www.theguardian.com/us-news/2018/may/19/stephen-paddock-las-vegas-shooter-conspiracy-theories-documents-explained

Chapter 4
Paper Terrorism and Other Tactics

Chapter four discusses paper terrorism, the term used to describe a common set of tactics used by sovereign citizens to retaliate against their perceived enemies. These tactics include the targeted harassment of public officials through the use of false liens, and other financially-oriented tactics, despite having no legal basis for doing so. A description of common schemes is presented below.

4.1 What Is Paper Terrorism?

When a sovereign citizen feels wronged, as they are prone to do, they commonly seek to retaliate against their perceived offender(s). As explained in chapter three, sometimes that retaliation includes violence. Paper-based revenge strategies often involve the filing of frivolous documents against perceived adversaries. Broadly speaking these tactics are referred to as paper terrorism. Paper terrorism is defined as the use of fraudulent legal documents and filings or the misuse of legitimate legal documents and filings. Judges, lawyers, law enforcement officers, county officials, and private citizens, have all been victims (Pitcavage 2012; Loeser 2015). Even the former IRS commissioner and its officials have been targets (Hodson 2019; Keneally 2013). No one is immune. Paper terrorism can also include tax schemes, forging documents, pyramid schemes, the creation of fake indictments, and the issuing of warrants against public officials (Bjelopera 2017).

The original version of this chapter was revised. The correction to this chapter is available at https://doi.org/10.1007/978-3-030-45851-5_8

© The Author(s), under exclusive license to Springer Nature
Switzerland AG 2020, Corrected Publication 2020
C. M. Sarteschi, *Sovereign Citizens*, SpringerBriefs in Psychology, https://doi.org/10.1007/978-3-030-45851-5_4

4.2 False Liens

A common form of paper terrorism involves filing liens. A lien (sometimes referred to as a commercial lien) is a legal claim on property for payment of a debt or obligation (Griffin and Runyon 2000, as cited in Chamberlain and Haider-Markel 2005). There are multiple types of liens, including the non-consensual, non-possessory which is a favorite among sovereign citizens. Often placed upon an unsuspecting victim without their knowledge, they are costly and time-consuming to remove (Chamberlain and Haider-Markel 2005). Left unchanged, they can negatively impact a victim's credit ratings and delay property sales (Snow 1999, as cited in Chamberlain and Haider-Markel 2005).

An example demonstrates how problematic liens can be. A South Carolina homeowner received a letter from the "Cherokee Nation of Moors." The author of the letter claimed that the city of Charlotte was the "Imperial city," that the "empire of the aboriginal Moors had been resurrected" and that all homes on the land, owed a "sovereign soil tax" of $500,000. The homeowner soon learned that a lien had been placed on her home and on the homes of three other people in the neighborhood. When the homeowner contacted the author of the letter (Empress Ninti El Bey, who had previously been convicted of trespassing and breaking and entering), she was threatened with a lawsuit. In investigating the problem further, the homeowner was told by the County Register of Deeds that "anyone can file a lien on a home as long as they paid the fee and fill out the paperwork properly… and you won't be notified." In order to fight the lien, the homeowner was told that she must hire an attorney to acquire a court order to have it removed (Wickersham 2018).

Fraudulent liens are also expensive for the government both in terms of time and money. Sovereign citizen cases often contain voluminous amounts of documents. Normal criminal cases have 60 or 70 court record entries whereas a typical sovereign citizen case may contain more than 1000 (March-Safbom 2018). Sorting through nonsensical documents is burdensome and costly to the court. Although many states have amended their lien laws to try to prevent these abuses, the outcomes have been marginal (McRoberts 2019).

The lien strategy is a preferred tactic among sovereign citizens in part because it is easy to accomplish, taking in some cases only minutes to fill out an online form (Lakin 2017). Anyone can file a lien under the Uniform Commercial Code (UCC) (Goode 2013) and many states have no pre-screening process (Crusco 2019). This is something the sovereign citizen knows and has weaponized against their perceived enemies. Consider the 74-page document entitled "Commercial Liens: A Most Potent Weapon" available via the internet. The document educates the reader about commercial liens. It says that they are simple, inexpensive, take very little time, require no court action or judge's approval, and can be filed on property in another state or on never-seen-before property. In addition, it reads, "with the commercial lien, you can attack the personal property of your adversary at long range. This offensive capacity makes the commercial lien a powerful legal weapon." Liens often contain demands for preposterous amounts of money, often in the millions or billions. The reason for this, according to the document, is to gain attention. Without those high dollar amounts, lien attempts might simply be ignored.

The New York Times recently highlighted the case of Minnesota Sheriff Richard Stanek. When attempting to refinance his mortgage, he learned that liens had been placed on his home and properties for more than $25 million. He subsequently learned that he had been one of more than a dozen victims of a sovereign citizen couple, angry about their 2009 home foreclosure. The couple had filed more than $250 billion in liens (Goode 2013). Court records indicate that they claimed to have received instructions about UCC filings from someone on the internet named "P.K." The couple said that P.K. instructed them to use the name "Blessings of Liberty" on the liens rather than their own names to protect themselves against criminal liability (*State of Minnesota v. Eilertson* 2015.). It was a preferred method of retaliation, P.K. told them, as it had the potential to "do death by 1000 paper cuts." The couple were prosecuted by Minnesota officials and sentenced to 23 months in prison and ordered to pay court fines (Young, 2013).

The National Association of Secretaries of State (NASS) recognize the problems associated with liens filed under the UCC. In 2014, a report acknowledged the dramatic rise in these filings. New York State, for instance, receives thousands of new UCC-1 filings each day (Crusco 2019). An important characteristic of sovereign citizen UCC filings, NASS noted in their report, is that the debtor is listed as a "transmitting utility." They explain that sovereign citizens recognize that transmitting utility filings never lapse thus ensuring that their financial statements remain indefinitely on file. Most UCC financing statements, NASS explains, lapse after five years from the date of filing.

NASS identifies two main types of fraudulent filings: harassment and straw man. Harassment filings involve retaliatory, false financing statements and property liens against government officials, corporations and banks. They note that judges, prosecutors and public defenders are also frequently targeted. A harassment filing involves a "debtor" supposedly owing large sums of money to the filer or the supposed "secured party." Harassment filings have become common among prison inmates who are able to easily to file these from an incarceration setting. A Pennsylvania State prison inmate convicted of rape filed retaliatory false liens seeking $56 million against the property of federal judges and other court officials involved in his case (Ove 2019). A federal jury convicted the inmate for the false liens and sentenced him to an additional four years (Ove 2019).

Straw man-type filings (also known as "redemption" or "accepted for value") involve the discredited idea that the federal government has dedicated accounts at the U.S. Treasury Department that contain anywhere from $600,000 to $3 million for citizens born in U.S. with a birth certificate. Sovereign citizens believe that filing UCC financing statements will allow access to these secret accounts.

An FBI alert describes instances in which trainers create "kits" to sell with the aim of teaching others how to perpetrate these schemes (n.d.). These trainers claim to have had great success with their efforts. Those who fail, they say, do so because they did not properly follow instructions (Federal Bureau of Investigation n.d.). Sovereign schemers utilize certain documents that appear legitimate but are fraudulent. These include "bills of exchange," "promissory bonds," "indemnity bonds," "offset bonds," "sight drafts," or "comptroller warrants" (Federal Bureau of Investigation n.d.).

Some sovereign citizens have also filed false IRS forms, tax returns, amended returns and Forms W-2 and 8300, in an attempt to acquire large tax returns they claim to be owed (Bjelopera 2017; Federal Bureau of Investigation n.d.). In one instance, a South Carolina dentist stopped sending her personal income tax returns and began mailing the IRS documents claiming she had the right not to file returns or pay taxes (ABC News 4 2018). Interestingly, Mark Pitcavage, of the Anti-Defamation League (ADL), notes that of March 2018, he had recorded 45 incidents involving dentists engaging in similar tactics (Pitcavage 2018).

4.3 OIDs and False Refund Cases

A common sovereign citizen scheme involves fraudulent "original issue discount" (OID) filings. These are legitimate IRS forms used for illegitimate purposes, also known as false refund cases (Ihlo and Pulice 2013). This scheme involves filing false tax returns using made up numbers based on the sovereign citizen's theory about redeeming money from the Treasury Department (i.e. redemption theory) (Ihlo and Pulice 2013). The IRS specifically warns about the established legal fact that "the Treasury Department does not contain depository counts against which an individual can draw a check, draft or any other financial instrument. The notion of secret accounts assigned each citizen is pure fantasy" (Internal Revenue Service 2018, p.46). Despite their repeated warnings, between 2012 and 2014, the IRS received nearly 7000 bogus OID filings (Powers 2019).

4.4 "Bond Process"

A 2019 *New York Times* article describes the case of Sean David Morton, a sovereign citizen "guru" known for promising, among other things, to reveal the secret "bond process" (Powers 2019). The bond process is simply another name of the "straw man," "redemption" or "accepted for value" schemes. He claimed, as do other sovereign citizens, that filing the right set of documents will wipe away all debts. Mr. Morton was a regular on the "Coast To Coast" radio program, at UFO conferences, and would often lecture at New Age centers, allowing him broad access to pitch his ideas to many people. He and his wife were eventually prosecuted on a number of charges related to his bond process scheme and improper tax returns. His wife was represented at trial by an attorney but Mr. Morton choose to represent himself. In his opening statement, he argued that he is "…not a rapist, a thug, a war criminal… I didn't run a Nazi concentration camp and murder millions of children." His closing statement focused on the fact that he and his wife had tried to rescue a premature kitten. He asked the jury to consider this question: "Do we send these nice people who care for kittens and raise cats to jail forever?" After two hours of deliberation, the jury verdict was guilty. Mr. Morton was sentenced to six years. He continues to file appeals from prison (Powers 2019).

Winston Shrout, another notorious sovereign citizen "guru," and recent fugitive, taught followers illegal schemes aimed at defrauding the U.S. Treasury and banks (Bernstein 2019). For instance, he claimed that court orders and money orders are the same thing and that federal judges use those orders to draw money from the Federal Reserve (McRoberts 2019). He admitted at trial to not having paid or filed an income tax return in over 20 years, despite earning over $500,000 (Bernstein 2019). Mr. Shrout is known for his many odd beliefs including his claim that he is an interplanetary diplomat, an "alien walk in" who inhabited a child's body, is descended from Jesus and Mary Magdalene, and was sent to earth "to destroy the Jesuits" (Bernstein 2018). Now captured, he is to serve a 10-year prison sentence (Bernstein 2019).

4.5 House Squatting

Some sovereign citizens believe that if a property is unclaimed, they have the right to live in it. They do this even though they have no legal rights to the land or property. For instance, Thomas Benson of Las Vegas conspired with his wife to take over a bank-owned home. The evicted tenants were called by Mr. Benson and told they could come back for their stuff (Segall 2016). When they arrived, all of their belongings were being removed by strangers. Mr. Benson subsequently sued for the property and a no trespassing sign and wooden barricades were placed in and around the home. Mr. Benson has a long history of engaging in fraudulent activities and has since been convicted for his crimes (Segall 2016).

Georgia has been a hotbed of sovereign citizen squatting activities. According to one news report, over half of all the vacant properties in Atlanta have squatters (Givens and King 2019). Sovereign squatters are known to carry firearms and be combative (Givens and King 2019). Sgt. Kory Flowers of the Greensboro Police Department has also observed an increase in squatting by Moorish sovereign citizens in North Carolina (Hanson 2015). The squatters are described as being assertive and aggressive. Law enforcement is often limited in how they can intervene. Sovereign citizens provide documentation "proving" they live in a particular residence. Though their documentation is fraudulent, Sgt. Flowers says that it is not the officer's job to determine its authenticity (Hanson 2015). Even when they are arrested, the squatters often return the very next day. Few good remedies exist for dealing with these ongoing issues.

4.6 Sovereign Citizen Fraud in U.S. Department of Housing and Urban Development (HUD) Programs

In 2015, the Office of Inspector General (OIG) issued a warning about sovereign citizens engaging in a number of scams including illegally occupying HUD properties, illegally deeding HUD-own properties to themselves, assuming ownership of the home, changing locks, and installing alarm systems. Sovereign citizens have also improperly rented out HUD-owned real estate to unsuspecting tenants, and participated in the HUD subsidize Sect. 8 Housing Choice Voucher program as landlords. They have also been able to convince defaulted homeowners to quit-claim their deeds by promising to stop the foreclosure. The sovereign citizen subsequently collects monthly payments from homeowners promising to return the deeds in the future. Victims of the scam are eventually evicted from their homes and face damaged credit. The Inspector General successfully secured approximately 20 convictions for HUD-related crimes, collecting more than $17 million in criminal recoveries (Office of Inspector General 2015).

4.7 Fraudulent Real Estate Ownership and Debt Elimination Services

In June 2019, the U.S. Department of Justice (DOJ) successfully prosecuted James Ignatius Diamond also known as "Jim Diamond" of Riverside, California for a fraudulent debt elimination scheme targeted at distressed homeowners, many of whom did not speak English well (Federal Bureau of Investigation 2018). His scheme involved a supposed loophole in the UCC code in which the homeowner could become the creditor and the financial institution/lender would become the debtor (Federal Bureau of Investigation 2018). During live seminars and presentations, Mr. Diamond told victims his programs would eliminate their debts altogether. Victims were asked to pay approximately $3500, plus additional program and notary fees. Prosecutors identified at least 500 victims totaling losses that exceeded $1.6 million (Federal Bureau of Investigation 2018). Mr. Diamond was convicted of 30 counts of mail fraud, and sentenced to nearly six years in prison.

4.8 Midwives and Private Membership Associations (PMAs)

In July of 2019, Kelly Weill of *The Daily Beast* documented two cases of unlicensed midwives whose clients' newborns died. In both cases, she found that the midwives were members of a "private membership association," a less common but bogus tactic associated with the sovereign citizen movement. Weill explained that members of the PMA claimed to be allowed to practice midwifery even though they were unlicensed. They contended that their membership in the PMA protected them against any legal liabilities.

In the first case, Angela Hock tried to unsuccessfully perform a breech birth during which the baby was without oxygen for 10 minutes resulting in death (Vigdor 2019). It is against the law in Nebraska for midwives to perform at-home births (Bandur 2019). Ms. Hock also indicated to the mother that she had training in certain types of birthing methods. She, in fact, had no training. On her website, she indicated that PMA members enjoy "general immunity to public laws, regulations, and internal rules of local, state and federal administrative agencies (including, but not limited to the FDA) that protect the public health" (Weill 2019). In a podcast after the incident, on an episode exploring the "undiscovered world of private membership associations" with midwife and trailblazer Angee Hock, Ms. Hock indicated that she "never wanted to be licensed because I don't like rules and regulations…" (Bandur 2019).

The second case described by Weill was that of an unlicensed midwife from Indiana named Julie Lenz. In this case, the mother's water had been broken for 10 days but Ms. Lenz talked her out of going to the hospital. When the mother eventually went to the hospital, she was diagnosed with a life-threatening infection and her baby died. Ms. Lenz also belonged to a PMA claiming that the "…midwife-client relationship is a private transaction that is outside the scope of public laws." J.J. MacNabb identified the PMA scam as a variation of what had previously been known as a "pure trust" or a "common-law trust." PMA's, MacNabb says, are not only used by midwives but also by others trying to avoid government regulations (Weill 2019).

4.9 Federal and State Laws Against Paper Terrorism

Sovereign citizens are known for their paper terrorism tactics. It is a difficult problem to resolve. The Southern Poverty Law Center (SPLC) indicates that as of 2017, there was only one federal law against criminal lien filings, only protecting federal judges, law enforcement officers, or employees of the U.S. (Paper terrorism 2017; Weir 2015). The passing of The Court Security Improvement Act of 2007 made it a federal crime to knowingly file or attempt to file false liens but it has been criticized as being too narrow. The law states that the filer must know or have a reason to know that the lien is false and the filing must have been motivated by retaliation against a government official (Weir 2015), both of which are difficult to prove. The narrowness of this law is exemplified by the rarity of its use (Weir 2015).

In their 2014 report, NASS identified four approaches to tackling the problem of fraudulent filings: (1) prefiling administrative discretion; (2) post-filing administrative relief; (3) post-filing expedited judicial relief; and (4) enhanced criminal/civil penalties. As of their 2014 report, every state had adopted some variation of these approaches. Though the most effective approaches are criminal penalties, only 15 states had criminalized the fraudulent filing of certain documents. In most cases, the first offense is a misdemeanor and subsequent offenses are felonies.

In a 2018 thesis about paper terrorism, March-Safbom (2018) observed a substantial expansion of all types of remedies. Regarding criminal penalties, 34 states had added criminal penalties to their existing statutes. March-Safbom (2018) also observed that 20 states charge fraudulent filings as felonies, with several states adding degree enhancements for subsequent charges. Despite the existence of federal and state laws, penalties vary and many sovereign citizens remain undeterred.

4.10 Profile of A Paper Terrorist

A profile of the paper terrorist may be emerging. Sullivan et al. (2019) compiled data from the U.S. Extremist Financial Crime Database (EFCD) to examine financial crimes among members of the far-right extremist movement (FRE), in the US. They focused on financial schemes carried out by a variety of individuals adhering to a FRE ideology. They analyzed a subset of individuals, including 215 schemes among 368 individual offenders between 2002 to 2004. They found that 126 individuals or 34% of the 215 schemes were committed by sovereign citizens. Demographically, offenders in their sample were mostly middle age, white males residing in the southern region of the U.S. The authors highlight the fact that some FREs have escalated into violence underscoring the need for more intervention and prevention strategies.

The case of Lee Harold Cromwell is one such example. He has a long history of paper assaults against public officials. His attacks escalated into violence when he drove his truck through a crowded parking lot at a 2015 fireworks celebration. He was convicted of reckless vehicular homicide and reckless aggravated assault against nine different victims and sentenced to 12 years. (Morlin 2018). During his trial, he and four other sovereign citizens filed millions of dollars' worth of liens against public officials involved in Mr. Cromwell's case. These liens led to additional criminal charges against Mr. Cromwell and his sovereign codefendants. The group of five were jointly prosecuted and convicted in what is considered "one of the largest joint prosecutions… ever undertaken in the United States" (Morlin 2018). The five men were sentenced to 20 to 50 years.

4.11 Conclusion

Sovereign citizens commit a variety of frivolous paper assaults. They are opportunistic schemers who have scammed many unsuspecting victims for the purpose of revenge and personal financial benefit. They have been engaging in these types of assaults for many years, yet relatively little has been done to effectively deter their efforts. States laws prohibit criminal false liens but most do not go far enough in effectively preventing paper terrorism. The fact remains that filing a false lien against an innocent and unsuspecting victim is remarkable easy. In the matter of minutes, and with the ease of the internet, anyone, even an incarcerated offender, can harass, intimidate or otherwise threaten any number of targets of their choosing. More safeguards are needed to prevent these troublesome acts.

References

ABC News 4. (2018, February 28). *SC dentist to join sovereign citizen tax protest movement sent to prison for tax crime*. Retrieved from https://abcnews4.com/news/crime-news/woman-sentenced-for-tax-violation

Bandur, M. (2019, July 4). Unlicensed midwife accused in newborn's death talked openly about skirting the law. *KETVOmaha*. Retrieved from https://www.ketv.com/article/unlicensed-midwife-accused-in-newborns-death-talked-openly-about-skirting-the-law/28287088

Bernstein, M. (2018, September 28). Tax dodger found competent for sentencing even with "alien" delusion. *The Oregonian*. Retrieved from https://www.oregonlive.com/portland/2018/09/man_who_failed_to_pay_taxes_fo_1.html

Bernstein, M. (2019, March 20). Prominent tax dodger now dodging prison sentence, prosecutor says. *The Oregonian*. Retrieved from https://www.oregonlive.com/crime/2019/03/tax-dodger-now-dodging-prison-sentence-prosecutor-says.html

Bjelopera, J. P. (2017). Domestic terrorism: An overview. Congressional Research Service. Retrieved from https://fas.org/blogs/secrecy/2017/08/domestic-terrorism-crs/

Chamberlain, R., & Haider-Markel, D. P. (2005). "Lien on me": State policy innovation in response to paper terrorism. *Political Research Quarterly, 58(3)*, 449–460. doi: 10.2307/3595614

Crusco, P. A. (2019, August 26). Sovereign foreclosures and the UCC-1 bogus lean scam. *New York Law Journal*. Retrieved from https://www.law.com/newyorklawjournal/2019/08/26/sovereign-foreclosures-and-the-ucc-1-bogus-lien-scam/?slreturn=20190928152611

Federal Bureau of Investigation. (2018, July 13). *Riverside Man and office manager indicted on federal charges alleging they operated a fraudulent debt-elimination scheme that targeted distressed homeowners during the housing crisis*. [Press release]. Retrieved from https://www.fbi.gov/contact-us/field-offices/losangeles/news/press-releases/riverside-man%2D%2Doffice-manager-indicted-on-federal-charges-alleging-they-operated-a-fraudulent-debt-elimination-scheme-that-targeted-distressed-homeowners-during-the-housing-crisis

Federal Bureau of Investigation. (n.d.). *Redemption/strawman/bond fraud*. Retrieved from https://www.fbi.gov/scams-and-safety/common-fraud-schemes/redemption-strawman-bond-fraud

Givens, L., & King, M. (2019, September 12). Realtor says squatting is becoming a greater problem across Georgia. *11Alive*. Retrieved from https://www.11alive.com/article/news/local/realtor-says-squatting-becoming-greater-problem/85-3f4740d1-5057-4988-90c9-99ef9ebdef0b

Goode, E. (2013, August 23). In paper war, flood of liens is the weapon. *The New York Times*. Retrieved from https://www.nytimes.com/2013/08/24/us/citizens-without-a-country-wage-battle-with-liens.html

Hanson, B. (2015). Fraud, squatting frequently link to 'Moorish' religion followers. *WSOC*. Retrieved from https://www.wsoctv.com/news/special-reports/fraud-squatting-frequently-linked-moorish-religion/26826407

Hodson, S. (2019, October 17). "Sovereign citizen" guilty on all 21 federal charges in a gusto trial. *The Augusta Chronicle*. Retrieved from https://www.augustachronicle.com/news/20191017/sovereign-citizen-guilty-on-all-21-federal-charges-in-augusta-trial

Ihlo, J. E., & Pulice, E. B. (2013). Prosecuting tax defier and sovereign citizen cases— Frequently asked questions. *United States Attorneys' Bulletin, 61*(2). Retrieved from https://www.justice.gov/sites/default/files/usao/legacy/2013/02/22/usab6102.pdf.

Internal Revenue Service. (2018). *The truth about frivolous tax arguments*. Retrieved from https://www.irs.gov/pub/taxpros/frivolous_truth_march_2018.pdf

Keneally, K. (2013). An introduction to the tax division. *United States Attorneys' Bulletin, 61*(2). Retrieved from https://www.justice.gov/sites/default/files/usao/legacy/2013/02/22/usab6102.pdf.

Lakin, M. (2017, March 19). Records: Bogus liens by East Tennessee "sovereign citizens" topped $2B. *Knoxville News Sentinel*. Retrieved from https://www.knoxnews.com/story/news/crime/2017/03/19/records-bogus-liens-sovereigns-topped-2-billion/99257156/

Loeser, C. E. (2015). From paper terrorists to cop killers: The sovereign citizen threat. *North Carolina Law Review., 93*(4), 1106–1139. Retrieved from http://scholarship.law.unc.edu/cgi/viewcontent.cgi?article=4744&context=.

March-Safbom T. (2018). Weapons of mass distraction: Strategies for countering the paper terrorism of sovereign citizens. *Homeland Security Affairs*.

McRoberts, C. (2019). Tinfoil hats and powdered wigs: Thoughts on pseudolaw. *Washburn Law Journal, 58*(3). Retrieved from https://ssrn.com/abstract=3400362.

Morlin, B. (2018). Five sovereign citizens convicted of fraud in Tennessee. *Southern Poverty Law Center*. Retrieved from https://www.splcenter.org/hatewatch/2018/05/08/five-sovereign-citizens-convicted-fraud-tennessee

National Association of Secretaries of State. (2014). *State strategies to subvert fraudulent uniform commercial code (UCC) filings: A report for state business filing agencies*. Retrieved from http://nass.org/sites/default/files/surveys/2017-08/final-nass-report-bogus-filings-040914.pdf

Office of Inspector General. (2015). Attention HUD REO contractors, property inspectors, section 8 administrators, and realtors: Watch out: Sovereign citizen scams. *The US Department of Housing and Urban Development*. Retrieved from https://www.hud.gov/sites/documents/SOVEREIGNCITIZENSCAMSV2.PDF

Ove, T. (2019, March 18). Pa. inmate gets more prison for filing false liens against Pittsburgh judges. *Pittsburgh Post-Gazette*. Retrieved from https://www.post-gazette.com/news/crime-courts/2019/03/18/pittsburgh-federal-judges-false-liens-clarence-hoffert-sentence-prison/stories/201903180117

Paper terrorism. (2017). *Southern Poverty Law Center*. Retrieved from https://www.splcenter.org/fighting-hate/intelligence-report/2017/paper-terrorism

Pitcavage, M. (2012). The lawless ones: The resurgence of the sovereign citizen movement. *Anti-Defamation League*. Retrieved from https://www.adl.org/sites/default/files/documents/assets/pdf/combating-hate/Lawless-Ones-2012-Edition-WEB-final.pdf

Pitcavage, M. [egavactip]. (2018, March 1). For some reason, dentists are vulnerable to getting wrapped up in sov cit & tax protest movements. I have a list of such incidents & she is now #45 on it. #45!! [Tweet]. Retrieved from https://twitter.com/egavactip/status/969337679052754945?lang=en

Powers, A. (2019, March 29). How sovereign citizens helped swindle $1 billion from the government they disavow. *The New York Times*. Retrieved from https://www.nytimes.com/2019/03/29/business/sovereign-citizens-financial-crime.html

Segall, E. (2016 November 27). 'Sovereign citizen' case reveals waters targeting vacant Las Vegas homes. *Las Vegas Review-Journal*. Retrieved from https://www.reviewjournal.com/business/housing/sovereign-citizen-case-reveals-squatters-targeting-vacant-las-vegas-homes/

State of Minnesota v. Eilertson. (2015). 62-CR-12-67. *State of Minnesota in Court of Appeals*.

References

Sullivan, B. A., Freilich, J. D., & Chermak, S. M. (2019). An examination of the american far right's anti-tax financial crimes. *Criminal Justice Review, 44*(4), 1–23.

Vigdor, N. (2019, July 6). Unlicensed Nebraska midwife is arrested in newborn's death after home delivery. *The New York Times*. Retrieved from https://www.nytimes.com/2019/07/06/us/nebraska-midwife.html

Weill, K. (2019, July 23). Two babies die in care of conspiracy-minded midwives. *The Daily Beast*. Retrieved from https://www.thedailybeast.com/two-babies-die-in-care-of-conspiracy-minded-midwives-who-belonged-to-pmas

Weir, J. P. (2015). Sovereign citizens: A reasoned response to the madness. *Lewis & Clark Law Review, 19(3)*, 829–870. Retrieved from https://law.lclark.edu/live/files/20846-lcb193art12weirpdf.

Wickersham, S. (2018, July 9). Home liens: 9 investigates: Liens placed on unsuspecting Charlotte homeowners, asks for $500K. *WSOC*. Retrieved from https://www.wsoctv.com/news/9-investigates/9-investigates-liens-placed-on-unsuspected-charlotte-homeowners-asks-for-500k/785040031

Young, J. (2013, June 10.). Former Brooklyn Park couple gets prison for $114 billion fraud scheme. *Sun Post*. Retrieved from: https://www.hometownsource.com/sun_post/news/public-safety/former-brooklyn-park-couple-gets-prison-for-billion-fraud-scheme/article_53cc30bd-ac31-594c-80bd-f0026fc35690.html

Chapter 5
Moors

Chapter five provides the reader with a general overview of a sovereign citizen-like movement called the Moors. The Moors subscribe to a different set of beliefs from those of sovereign citizens but use similar tactics. Their rationale for breaking the law or evading the law is different from that of the typical sovereign citizen but they behave in a very similar way. A description of Moors, their beliefs, their behavior, their interactions with public officials, law enforcement officers and the American judicial system are described below.

Within the sovereign citizen movement exists an off-shoot of individuals who are commonly referred to as Moors (sometimes spelled Muurs). The Moorish sovereign citizen movement is thought to have largely started in the 1990s in East coast cities (Pitcavage, as cited in Moorish sovereign citizens n.d.; Parker 2018). Some have described the beliefs of the sovereign Moors to be a combination of more typical sovereign citizens beliefs (rejecting government authority) with that of the Moorish Science Temple of America (MSTA), a religious sect founded in 1913 by Noble Drew Ali, who considered himself a prophet. Some Moors have also adopted ideas from the Louisiana-based Washitaw Nation, a small group who claims that they are sovereign entities and as such do not have to follow the laws of the U.S. (Parker 2018; Federal Bureau of Investigation 2017). Researchers have indicated that there is no published estimate of the number of sovereign Moors currently in existence in the US (Parker 2018).

The extant research about Moorish sovereign citizens is extremely limited. A review of the literature indicates that there are only two scholarly articles that specifically examine Moorish sovereigns (i.e. Parker 2018 and Dew 2016). One additional article (i.e. Bailey 2006) could be located which focuses on the United Nuwaubian Nation of Moors, which the Southern Poverty Law Center (SPLC) categorizes as a

---

The original version of this chapter was revised. The correction to this chapter is available at https://doi.org/10.1007/978-3-030-45851-5_8

© The Author(s), under exclusive license to Springer Nature Switzerland AG 2020, Corrected Publication 2020
C. M. Sarteschi, *Sovereign Citizens*, SpringerBriefs in Psychology, https://doi.org/10.1007/978-3-030-45851-5_5

black nationalist group, that has adopted some of the Moorish sovereign tactics. Most information about Moorish sovereign citizens, and sovereign citizens in general, comes from the law enforcement sources, the SPLC, the Anti-Defamation League (ADL), media reporting, typically about illegal actions by Moorish sovereign citizens, and court documents. The SPLC (n.d.) explicitly states that the origins of the Moorish sovereign citizen movement are "difficult to ascertain."

Spencer Dew (2016) traced the history of the MSTA. He includes a thorough analysis of several Moorish sovereign gurus who have intermixed sovereign citizen ideology with MSTA ideas and are teaching it to their followers. The intermixing of these ideas has led to confusion as to who are the legitimate members of the MSTA and who are those claiming to be legitimate but who are, in actuality, Moorish sovereigns. In 2011, the MSTA home office, located in Washington D.C., issued a statement condemning the practices of "radical and subversive fringe groups claiming to be affiliated" with the MSTA. The statement read (in part) that: "some people are under the misconception and erroneous notion that the Moorish Science Temple of America, Inc. is a place where one can learn how to forgo their civic duty of paying taxes, obtain their 'straw-man,' and assert their so-called sovereignty, etc. We assertively declare that the Moorish Science Temple of America, Inc. is in no form or fashion a Sovereign Citizen Movement or a Tax Protester Movement, consequently our teachings are diametrically opposed to that ideology" (NBC Washington 2017, para 16).

Members of the MSTA Georgia office followed suit, referring to Moorish sovereign citizen claims as being "completely asinine" (*Bey v. State of Indiana* 2017). Their website describes how to recognize fake or bootleg MSTA temples. The fake ones, they say, can be spotted when there is any mention of the following: "paperwork to file in the court; straw-man to claim; natural person to proclaim, UCC or naturalization documents; right-to-road travel; sovereignty or indigenous status; peace and friendship treaty; jurisdictional status; Mason or Kemetic science teachings; Dr. York or C.M. Bey teachings or zodiac or astrology teachings." They describe, on their website, in greater detail, the best ways to discern the difference between legitimate and illegitimate MSTA teachings. They have taken on the task of defending against the "so-called Moorish Sovereignty, Moorish Federation, Moorish Indigenous person, and the Moorish Republic" by acting as the "vanguards defending against bogus claims, lewd acts and sheer lawlessness of those who continue to set themselves as a threat to our peaceful way of living." The SPLC identified additional Moorish sovereign citizen groups including: the Free Moorish Nation, the United Mawshakh nation of Nuurs, the Nuwaubian Nation of Moors and the Al Moroccan Empire (Moorish sovereign citizens n.d.).

5.1 Origins of the Moors

The early Moorish science teachings of Drew Ali emphasized spirituality, the importance and responsibilities of citizenship, particularly in the form of voting. Nelson (2011) explains that Drew Ali taught his followers that the Earth's original single continent, Amexem, was entirely inhabited by Moors, individuals of north

African Berber and Arab dissent (Federal Bureau of Investigation 2017). A massive earthquake split the continent, creating the Atlantic Ocean, and the Americas. Those first inhabitants were the Moors, insists Drew Ali, who were here long before all other people (Nelson 2011). Nelson (2011) explains that Drew Ali believed that God had sent European colonists to enslave the Moors for having forgotten their history. The only way to reclaim their heritage, according to Drew Ali, was to differentiate themselves from slaves. To ensure government "recognition and respect as full citizens rather than second-class descendants of slaves" he encouraged his followers to refer to themselves as Moors, as opposed to "black," "African-American" and "colored" (Nelson 2011).

After the death of Drew Ali in 1929, the group devolved into competing factions. Legal battles ensued. Dew (2016) notes that it is often the case that MSTA adherents and Moorish sovereigns both "draw their authority from the same writings– and often from the same passages" (p.76). Though they may be reading from the same religious writings, their interpretations are vastly different. True MSTA adherents believe in the rule of law whereas Moorish sovereigns, in their attempts to interpret the historical teachings of Drew Ali, advise their followers to break the law in a variety of ways. Drew Ali encouraged his members to "see the duty and wisdom of at all times upholding… obedience to law, respect and loyalty to government," and "not to use any assertion against the American flag" (Nelson 2011, para. 21). Moorish sovereigns, alternatively, operate from the perspective of there being "only one true law," which only they understand, and which supersedes the legal knowledge of others (Dew 2016, p. 91), including licensed legal officials.

5.2 Moorish Sovereigns

Contemporary Moorish sovereign citizen claims include the belief that there exists a 1787 treaty between U.S. and Morocco that grants them immunity from the U.S. law. The Washitaw Nation, said to be one of the earliest Moorish sovereign citizen groups that began intermixing Moorish science teachings with sovereign citizen concepts, falsely claims to occupy United Nations Indigenous People's Seat 215, which they believe affords them the authority to create their own birth certificates, passports, driver's licenses, and vehicle registrations (Moorish sovereign citizens n.d.). According to the SPLC, none of the aforementioned claims are true. The FBI (2017) has also indicated that some Moorish sovereigns attempt to assert diplomatic immunity by claiming to be members of fictitious North American tribes, who are allegedly descendants of settlers who arrived in North America during the pre-Columbian era. Some also illegally identify themselves as foreign nationals or ambassadors.

Dew (2016) explains that Moorish sovereign thinkers interpret Drew Ali's writings in ways that encourage followers to break the law. Their teachings are centered on three main themes: (1) interpreting the fourteenth amendment to indicate that it gives a Moor an "artificial citizen" or "straw man" status; (2) the use of dictionaries to substantiate claims, one favorite being Black's Law Dictionary; and (3) providing Moors with supposed expert legal advice to use with law enforcement and in court. Dew (2016) describes one sovereign thinker who specifically indicated that sovereign Moorish nationals are not bound by any laws whatsoever. This particular Moor includes documentation at the end of his book, encouraging its use for legal purposes.

Other common Moorish sovereign teachings, according to Dew (2016), involve the following ideas: that the U.S. government lacks jurisdiction, and that major events in the 1930s, including the stock market crash and the Great Depression, allowed the Illuminati to overthrow the government and replace it with the "Corporate United States of America." Subsequently, the Constitution was revoked and "perpetual Maritime law" went into effect. As of 1933, the story goes, the Constitution was no longer recognized and was replaced by "color-of-law" and "private law."

The birth certificate is of particular importance to the Moorish sovereign citizen. It proves an individual's "corporate status" as demonstrated by the fact that one's name is written in all capital letters. These capital letters indicate a fictitious name, a "straw man," and thus not one's true name. Only small letters represent the real person, the "flesh-and-blood person." In order to remedy this, one is advised to change their name through the filing of certain documents including a "Proclamation of Nationality and Birthright" and a "Declaration of Nationality" which allegedly allows an individual the "[r]ight to travel, proclaiming indigenous/Moorish status, dual citizenship, jurisdiction, positive identification, and domicile" (Dew 2016, p.82). Should one be questioned about their right to travel, and have to defend themselves to law enforcement or in court, some Moorish sovereign teachings provide specific remedies for such matters. That aforementioned information is being taught via in-person seminars, complete with live simulations, for a fee (Moorish sovereign citizens n.d.; Dew 2016).

In addition to the belief that they are immune from all laws, Moorish sovereigns are known for refusing to pay taxes, registering their vehicles illegally, squatting in foreclosed or abandoned homes, mortgage fraud, and attempting to defraud banks and institutions (Moorish sovereign citizens n.d.; A Quick Guide to Sovereign Citizens 2012). Two ways to identify Moorish sovereign citizens are their use of red emblems or thumbprints on legal filings and the inclusion of "Bey" or "El" in their names (Moorish sovereign citizens n.d.). Men often wear hats called a Fez, commonly associated with Morocco (Koura 2017). Women often wear a turban and loose-fitting clothing (Koura 2017). Acquiring a marriage license is ill-advised, according to some Moorish sovereigns, and attempts should be made to terminate one's social security number (Dew 2016). It should be noted that there is no evidence that any of these tactics work. Alternatively, there is plenty of evidence indicating that these tactics are wholly ineffective, often leading to civil and criminal sanctions.

Frequently, cases involving Moorish sovereign citizen arguments are dismissed by the courts. Case in point: a Moorish sovereign was convicted of armed robbery and felony firearms charges. He was sentenced to over 40 years in prison. He filed a complaint with the court in which he claimed to be "controlled only by admiralty law and the Uniform Crime Code," that his arrest warrant was exercised against a "legal fiction commercial name in caps… without a security-for-performance bond, as required for maritime and bankruptcy liens." He also argued that the court lacked jurisdiction over his case. He was seeking relief from his imprisonment. Judge Paul Maloney correctly identified his claims as being sovereign citizen in nature, writing that "the capitalization of Plaintiff's name did not create a fictitious legal entity, and it certainly did not turn such artificial entity into property governed by the Uniform Commercial Code or admiralty law. The courts repeatedly have rejected such "redemptionalist and sovereign citizen" arguments as utterly frivolous." Like many others making similar claims, the case was dismissed (*Muhammad v. Michigan Department of Corrections* et al. 2017).

5.3 Moorish Sovereigns and Their Association With Other Groups

According to the FBI (2017), some individuals who ascribe to Moorish sovereign citizen ideology have been linked to the black identity extremists (BIE) movement. The Office of Homeland Security and Preparedness in the state of New Jersey refers to this overlapping between the two groups as "blended extremists" and believe that they present a unique threat (New Jersey Office of Homeland Security and Preparedness 2016). In their assessment of the threat, the FBI contend that the convergence of the BIE and Moorish sovereign citizen ideology "very likely leads to violence against law enforcement officers" (p.4). That was judged to be the case in four of the six BIE attacks against law enforcement since 2014, perpetrators were motivated by a mix of the two ideologies. It should be noted that Christopher Wray, director of the FBI, announced in an April 2019 Senate Judiciary hearing that the agency no longer uses the BIE label (Booker 2019). Critics argued, most prominently, Senator Cory Booker, that the use of the term unfairly targeted black activists and protesters (Booker 2019), particularly the group Black Lives Matter (BLM) (Speri 2019). It is unclear how the FBI currently tracks these threats.

The SPLC also indicates that Moorish sovereigns have been known to affiliate with black nationalist groups and notorious criminal gangs including the Bloods street gang, the Latin Kings street gang, the new Black Panther Party, the Nation of Islam, and black Hebrew Israelites (Moorish sovereign citizens n.d.). The SPLC has observed that some Moorish sovereign citizens have modified their vehicles to resemble police patrol cars and have been known to wear uniformed clothing with patches of the Moorish flag (Moorish sovereign citizens n.d.). One Moorish group, who refers to themselves as the Moorish American Consulate, is selling T-shirts reading "Sharifian Peace Officer." According to the website, only individuals who have been appointed as peace officers are allowed to issue orders. It is not clear what exactly constitutes a peace officer and what supposed powers they have.

5.4 The Nuwaubian Nation of Moors

Bailey (2006) documents the rise and fall of the United Nuwaubian Nation of Moors, a group that has been referred to as a cult but who regard themselves as being a "fraternal organization" of a variety of different religions (Monroe/Eatonton 1999). The group took up residence in Putnam, Georgia in 1997, after the purchase of land in the state. Upon their arrival from Brooklyn, New York, they constructed a number of pyramids, including a 40-foot-high black pyramid, along with a number of other statutes of ancient Egyptian gods and goddesses. The leader and founder of the movement is Dwight "Malachi" York (also known as Isa Muhammad, Alihad Mahdi and "Baba") (WMAZ 2018). He has written prolifically in the areas of psychology, telepathy, physics, and extraterrestrials (Bailey 2006). The group holds unconventional beliefs such as their leader is an extraterrestrial being from the galaxy Illyuwn. They also prophesized that a spaceship from the planet Rizq would return on May 5, 2003 to collect true believers (Monroe/Eatonton 1999). Wesley Snipes was once thought to be an active member of the group (Bailey 2006).

Upon relocating to Georgia, the group began having problems with the local authorities, namely Sheriff Howard Sills. In response to what they saw as unfair treatment, the group slandered government officials, threatened leaders and disrupted community meetings (Moorish sovereign citizens n.d.). Sheriff Sills also received a number of anonymous death threats (Moorish sovereign citizens n.d.). Local law enforcement had begun referring to their living quarters, known as "Tama-Re," as a "compound." FBI reports indicated that a number of the group's members have links to crime such as welfare fraud and extortion. Mr. York himself has an extensive criminal history including statutory rape, among other charges, and is now serving 135-year sentence for federal child molestation.

The group regards themselves as original Native Americans and declared themselves sovereigns (Bailey 2006). Much like other sovereign citizens, they issue their own passports and other legal paperwork. They also have an organized armed private security unit to protect their land (Bailey 2006). In court, Mr. York utilized common Moorish sovereign citizen tactics. For instance, he would not allow court officials to say his name during the trial and claimed to be "secured" (Bailey 2006). Members of the media were given a "copyright notice" that his name and aliases could not be used without his expressed permission or else financial penalties would be imposed. The copyright notice was allegedly issued by the "Clerk of Federal Moorish Cherokee Consular Court, USA" of which no such entity exists (Bailey 2006, p.314). Mr. York also claimed immunity explaining himself to be a sovereign Indian chief who is not subject to federal law. He asked the court to declare him as an indigenous person, a Moorish Cherokee who had "an alienable right to be tried by my own people" and stated that he was under duress when he plead guilty (Bailey 2006, p.314). In 2018, Mr. York filed a $2 billion lawsuit demanding compensation from government agencies and asserting that as a Native American, the U.S. has no legal jurisdiction over him (WMAZ 2018). In the lawsuit, he cites an 1871 statute that says that people have the right to sue local governments for civil rights violations (WMAZ 2018). He is currently housed at the infamous U.S. Penitentiary Administrative Maximum Facility (ADX) and is not scheduled for release from federal prison until the year 2122 (Forsythe 2019).

Despite their leader being incarcerated, there remain individuals claiming membership in the group, some of whom are alleged to have committed violent crimes. For instance, Rameses Richardson, also known as Quincy Richardson and Prince York, was arrested on March 10, 2019 for abusing the son of his girlfriend. News reports have indicated that on his Facebook page, Prince York describes himself as "one of the most inspirational public figures in our community…" and comments about how his father has been the subject of false charges at the hands of the state of Georgia (Conte 2017). In another instance, Calvin McIntosh, who self-identified as a member of the Moors, pled guilty to the 2014 starving death of his infant daughter and sentenced to life in prison (Sharpe 2018).

5.5 Islamic State in Iraq and Syria (ISIS)

Some researchers have speculated that ISIS may have been attempting to recruit Moorish sovereign citizens during a 2014 Ferguson protest (MacNab 2018). A *Washington Post* report indicated that ISIS appeared to have been using the Ferguson protest to encourage it supporters to carry out attacks in the U.S. In a tweet that was translated from a known Islamic state terrorist, it read "O supporters of the Islamic State in America, what is happening in #Ferguson is a valuable opportunity that will not return. Rise up and engage them with themselves, away from the mujahideen. Spill their blood in the roads and in the neighborhoods" (Itkowitzm 2014). In media reports after the event, Steve Wigginton, the U.S. Attorney in the Southern District of Illinois, indicated that his office had received confirmation from federal law enforcement officials that ISIS was encouraging people to join those who were burning buildings in Ferguson and to carry out similar attacks throughout the U.S. (KSDK 2014). It was the opinion of the U.S. attorney that ISIS was "trying to reach the people who are antigovernment to begin with… whether they are sovereign citizens…[or]… anarchists… They all showed up at one point or another in the St. Louis area in the last few months" (KSDK 2014). Relatedly, Arizona sovereign citizen Abdul Khabir Wahid was connected to Islamist extremists who shot at protesters attending a free-speech rally in Texas. Though he was not directly involved in the attack, Mr. Wahid was convicted of making a false statement to the FBI regarding his delivering a key to individuals involved in the shooting (United States Department of Justice 2019). Confirmation about whether ISIS had definitively attempted to recruit Moorish sovereign citizens, or sovereign citizens in general, is not available.

5.6 Scientology and the Anti-Vaccination Movement

Ortega (2019) identified a case of well-known Scientologists using Moorish sovereign citizen tactics in court. Hanan Islam, executive director the World Literacy Crusade, three of her adult children, and a number of other associates, are accused of running a multimillion-dollar insurance scam involving a Scientology-based drug rehabilitation center in Compton, California. In a recent hearing, Hanan and her son Rizza (who, according to a post on his Facebook page, is the nephew of the rapper Snoop Dogg) attempted the "straw man" argument, insisting that their fictional corporate entities were on trial, and not their "natural" selves (Ortega 2019). Rizza Islam also appears to be against vaccinations. He indicated in a September 2019 Twitter post that "some of the vaccines that #America is forcing onto people specifically in CA right now are the same vaccines that were causing nearly 5000 children to die every week in Harare, #Zimbabwe…" In an earlier Instagram post from April 2019, he advertised a film screening and panel discussion regarding the "demonic genocidal system called #vaccines." That panel was set to take place at a university in Alabama, and involve Dr. Andrew Wakefield, the discredited ex-physician who lost his medical license after falsely linking the measles, mumps and rubella (MMR) vaccine to autism (Quick and Larson 2018). As of September 2019, Ortega (2019) reported that both defendants tried to fire the judge in their case. After more problematic antics in the courtroom, both were arrested for contempt of court and sentenced to five days in jail and fined $1000 (Ortega 2019). The case against Hanan and Rizza is still pending.

5.7 Violence Toward Law Enforcement By Moorish Sovereign Citizens

Moorish sovereign citizens are known for their acts of paper terrorism, a topic discussed in the previous chapter. Some have also committed extreme acts of violence toward police. Everett Glenn Miller, who went by the name Malika Muhammad Ali on Facebook, shot and killed two Florida police officers on August 18, 2017. In a post on social media, he proclaimed himself a Moor. To establish the connection, an expert testified about his use of the hashtag #makeamerickkamooragain, his requesting books from relatives about black superiority and finding handwritten notes in his car referencing Moorish leaders (Kelly and Deal 2018). Prior to the shooting, he had written about his anger about racism in the U.S., slavery, the KKK, and the events in Charlottesville (McBride 2017). Mr. Miller is thought to have ambushed the officers, purposefully interacting with them in order to shoot them (Cordeiro 2019a). After he shot the officers in the head, Mr. Miller fled the scene and drove to a bar and was later arrested. His social media comments, and his identification as a Moorish sovereign citizen, were prominently featured in his prosecution. After two hours, a jury found him guilty and as of the time of this writing, he was facing the death penalty (Corderio 2019b).

5.7 Violence Toward Law Enforcement By Moorish Sovereign Citizens

A high-profile case of violence involving a Moorish sovereign citizen is that of Eugene Gavin Long. On July 17, 2016, Mr. Long traveled from Kansas City, Missouri to Baton Rouge, Louisiana and shot six law enforcement officers. He attacked the officers ambush-style. Mr. Long was subsequently shot and killed by a Special Weapons and Tactics (SWAT) team. In addition to believing that he was a targeted individual (TI), Mr. Long identified himself on various social media accounts as being a member of the Washitaw Nation, also known as the Washitaw de Dugdahmoundyah (Sarteschi 2018). The Washitaw Nation was founded by Verdiacee Hampton Goston, self-proclaimed "empress," also known as Veridace Turner and Empress Verdiacee Turner Goston El-Bey (Bolden and Lenox 2016). The group claims sovereignty over 30 million acres in Louisiana, and parts of Arkansas and Mississippi (Martin 2014). The group contends that they are exempt from all U.S. laws, do not have to pay taxes, and are able to create their own laws, legal system and government (Bolden and Lenox 2016). After the shooting by Mr. Long, a representative for the Nation claims not to have known the shooter. Even though nationality paperwork and an ID were found in his possession, the group indicated that these materials were "sold to him by a fraudulent Washitaw group out of North Carolina called Unity Washitaw led by an impostor who operates strictly on material gain" (Bolden and Lenox 2016). U.S. courts, as well as the SPLC, regard the Washitaw Nation as a "fictitious" group (Martin 2014). Much like Everett Glenn Miller, it is believed that Mr. Long was driven to target law enforcement officers, in part, because of his anger about the police shootings of African American males (Sarteschi 2018).

Additional cases involving Moorish sovereigns include the following:

- In 2018, Tierre Guthrie, a known Moorish sovereign, was being served an arrest warrant and was not cooperating with police. After attempting to force him out of his home, Guthrie began shooting at police officers, hitting at least three of them. Officer Chase Maddox was shot in the head and died. The others were saved by bullet-proof vests. Individuals who knew Mr. Guthrie, a former Marine, said that he did not recognize the right of deputies to be on his property, did not trust doctors, did not allow his wife to work, and homeschooled his children because he did not trust educators (Boone and Stafford 2018).
- Yahchanan Christopher Reames, shot two deputies during a traffic stop in Bishopville, South Carolina. Both officers were wearing bulletproof vests and sustained non-life-threatening injuries. Mr. Reames was shot in the arm by police officers (Man Accused of Shooting Deputies 2013). At the time of the shooting, Mr. Reames had been out on bond for having attempted to fight police officers during a prior traffic stop (MacNab 2014). Since his conviction, Reames has continued to file many nonsensical motions with the court.
- James Michael Tesi of the "Moorish National Republic" (also known as House of Tesi or James Michael Joseph Tesi El) was convicted of aggravated assault of a public servant with a deadly weapon and sentenced to 35 years in prison. He shot an officer during a traffic stop in 2011. The officer was shot in the leg and survived (*Tesi v. The State of Texas* 2014). Mr. Tesi had previously been stopped

for driving without a seatbelt, refused to pay the fine and an arrest warrant was issued. He was again stopped for speeding and refusing to produce a driver's license and was subsequently arrested for a previous warrant.

At their core, Moorish sovereigns have much in common with typical sovereign citizens. Both reject government authority, deny the legitimacy of the legal and judicial systems in the U.S. and are willing to engage in violent acts in furtherance of their beliefs. The main difference between the two are their fundamental belief systems. Many Moorish sovereigns believe that they were the first inhabitants in America. This status provides them with special privileges, namely immunity from all U.S. government laws, not having to pay taxes, acquire a driver's license or a car registration, and a belief that each person has two identities, a real person and a fictional person, called the "straw man," the latter of which has been repeatedly rejected by the courts as being frivolous. The content of their beliefs, much like more typical sovereign citizens, is odd and can vary. To date, very little research exists about Moorish sovereign citizens. More work is necessary to understand the nature of their claims, and, most importantly, how to prevent their continued rejection of government authority and violence towards law enforcement and others in the community.

References

A quick guide to sovereign citizens. (2012). *University of North Carolina at Chapel Hill School of Government*. Retrieved from https://www.sog.unc.edu/sites/www.sog.unc.edu/files/additional_files/Sovereign%20citizens%20briefing%20paper%20Nov

Bailey, J. H. (2006). The final frontier: Secrecy, identity, and the media in the rise and fall of the United Nuwaubian Nation of Moors. *Journal of the American Academy of Religion, 74(2)*, 302–323. doi: https://doi.org/10.1093/jaarel/lfj085

Bey v. State of Indiana. (2017). No. 16–1589. *Court of Appeals for the Seventh Circuit*.

Bolden, B., & Lenox, B. (2016, July 18). B.R. shooter unknown to son of Washitaw Nation head. *The News Star*. Retrieved from https://wlna-webservice.gannettdigital.com/articleservice/view/87246606/michigan-state-spartans/24.3.57/iphone?apiKey=57646bc6bca4811fea00000126a000bb69414f2a44f75039173cf104

Booker, C. (2019, July 23). *Video: in response to Booker questioning, FBI director announces agency no longer uses baseless "black identity extremists" labels*. [Press release]. Retrieved from https://www.booker.senate.gov/?p=press_release&id=965

Boone, C., & Stafford, L. (2018, February 10). Shooter who allegedly killed one cop, injured two deputies was an ex-Marine. *The Atlanta Journal-Constitution*. Retrieved from https://www.ajc.com/news/shooter-who-killed-one-cop-injured-two-deputies-marine/RVs1tMt2bCxhZzAspRqdkL/#

Conte, M. (2017, March 22). Man charged with child abuse is son of black supremacist cult leader serving 135 years. *The Jersey Journal*. Retrieved from https://www.nj.com/hudson/2017/03/father_of_jersey_city_man_charged_with_child_abuse.html.

Cordeiro, M. (2019a, August 30a). Everett Miller trial: Marine veteran was in 'downward spiral' before fatal shooting of 2 Kissimmee cops. *Orlando Sentinel*. Retrieved from https://www.orlandosentinel.com/news/crime/os-ne-everett-miller-trial-opening-statements-20190830-pw6ueibcine5hgdwv7vufooxhy-story.html

References

Cordeiro, M. (2019b, August 30b). Everett Miller verdicts: guilty of 1st-degree murder in killing of 2 Kissimmee cops. *Orlando Sentinel*. Retrieved from https://www.orlandosentinel.com/news/crime/os-ne-jurors-deliberate-everett-miller-trial-20190911-muuxaslajjcyjj57jd35q6r64i-story.html

Dew, S. (2016). Moors know the law: Sovereign legal discourse in Moorish science religious communities and the hermeneutics of supersession. *Journal of Law and Religion, 31*(1), 1–22. https://doi.org/10.1017/jlr.2016.3.

Federal Bureau of Investigation. (2017). *Black identity extremists likely motivated to target law enforcement officers*. Washington, DC: Federal Bureau of Investigation, Counterterrorism Division.

Forsythe, J. (2019, August 12). The 14 most notorious inmates at the ADX in Florence, Colorado. *5280*. Retrieved from: https://www.5280.com/2019/08/the-14-most-notorious-inmates-at-the-adx-in-florence-colorado/

Itkowitz, C. (2014, November 25). Ferguson protest used as fuel for Islamic state propaganda. *The Washington Post*. Retrieved from https://www.washingtonpost.com/blogs/in-the-loop/wp/2014/11/25/ferguson-protests-used-as-fuel-for-islamic-state-propaganda/

Kelly, J. & Deal, J. (2018, September 18). Eyewitness: man accused of killing two Kissimmee officers might be linked to extremist group. *WFTV9ABC*. Retrieved from https://www.wftv.com/news/local/expert-witness-man-accused-of-killing-2-kissimmee-officers-might-be-linked-to-extremist-group/836546823

Koura, C. (2017, May 27). The American Religion That Makes Its Members "Moroccans." *Morocco World News*. Retrieved from https://www.moroccoworldnews.com/2017/05/217826/the-american-religion-that-makes-it-members-moroccans/

KSDK. (2014, December 23). *ISIS tries to influence criminals in Ferguson*. Retrieved from https://www.ksdk.com/article/news/local/ferguson/isis-tries-to-influence-criminals-in-ferguson/63-211169220

MacNab. J.J. (2014, October 10). As pressure mounts to 'demilitarize' police, sovereign citizens arm for war. *Forbes*. Retrieved from https://www.forbes.com/sites/jjmacnab/2014/10/10/sovereign-citizens-prepare-for-war-as-pressure-mounts-to-demilitarize-police/#343e88a37be8

MacNab, J.J. ([jjmacnab). (2018, July 10). According to the DOJ, ISIS try to recruit sovereign citizens at the 2014 Ferguson protest. My guess is that they were Moorish sovereigns. [Tweet]. Retrieved from https://twitter.com/jjmacnab/status/1016749958949527552

Man accused of shooting deputies was out of jail on bond. (2013, December 19). *WISNEWS*. Retrieved from https://www.wistv.com/story/24264715/two-lee-co-deputies-shot/

Martin, J. (2014, May 2). Recalling the FBI raid of the late Washitaw Nation leader's home. *The Franklin Sun*. Retrieved from https://www.hannapub.com/franklinsun/recalling-the-fbi-raid-of-late-washitaw-nation-leader-s/article_de819b14-d233-11e3-91b9-001a4bcf6878.html

McBride, J. (2017, August 19). Everett Glenn Miller: 5 fast facts you need to know. *Heavy*. Retrieved, from https://heavy.com/news/2017/08/everett-glenn-miller-kissimmee-glen-suspect-police-shot-shooting-matthew-baxter-sam-howard-photos-facebook/

Monroe/Eatonton, S. (1999, July 4). Space invaders. *Time*. Retrieved from http://content.time.com/time/magazine/article/0,9171,27708,00.html

Moorish sovereign citizens. (n.d.). *Southern Poverty Law Center*. Retrieved from https://www.splcenter.org/fighting-hate/extremist-files/group/Moorish-sovereign-citizens

Muhammad v Michigan Department of Corrections et al. (2017). 1:17-cv-68. *United States District Court for the Western District of Michigan Southern Division*.

NBC Washington. (2017, December 1). *Moorish nationalist couple arrested again for trying to claim rights to a DC home: Police*. Retrieved from https://www.nbcwashington.com/news/local/Moorish-Nationalist-Couple-Arrested-Again-for-Trying-to-Claim-Rights-to-a-DC-Home-461184553.html

Nelson, L. (2011). 'Sovereigns 'in black." *Southern Poverty Law Center*. Retrieved from https://www.splcenter.org/fighting-hate/intelligence-report/2011/%E2%80%98sovereigns%E2%80%99-black

New Jersey Office of Homeland Security and Preparedness. (2016). *Overlap between black separatists and Moorish sovereign citizen extremists*. Retrieved from https://www.njhomelandsecurity.gov/analysis/overlap-between-black-separatists-and-Moorish-sovereign-citizen-extremists

Ortega, T. (2019 September 18). Scientologist facing felonies try 'sovereign citizen' gambit in tense L.A. court hearing. *The Underground Bunker*. Retrieved from https://tonyortega.org/2019/09/18/scientologists-facing-felonies-try-sovereign-citizen-gambit-in-tense-la-court-hearing/

Parker, G. F. (2018). Sovereign citizens and competency to stand trial. *The Journal of the American Academy of Psychiatry and the Law, 46*(2), 4. https://doi.org/10.29158/JAAPL.003743-18.

Quick. J. D., & Larson, H. (2018, February 28). The vaccine autism myth started 20 years ago today. Here's why it's still endorsed today. *Time*. Retrieved from https://time.com/5175704/andrew-wakefield-vaccine-autism/

Sarteschi, C. M. (2018). Mass murder, targeted individuals, and gang stalking: Exploring the connection. *Violence and Gender, 5*(1), 45–54. https://doi.org/10.1089/vio.2017.0022.

Sharpe, J. (2018, September 18). Man enters plea in Gwinnett Bay be starving death-- but still disputes case. *The Atlantic Journal-Constitution*. Retrieved from https://www.ajc.com/news/local/breaking-surprise-guilty-plea-gwinnett-cult-baby-starving-death/mUAV0qvqI3mtuzF5UOltxM/

Speri, A. (2019, March 23). Fear of a black homeland: The strange tale of the FBI's fictional "black identity extremism" movement. *The intercept*. Retrieved from https://theintercept.com/2019/03/23/black-identity-extremist-fbi-domestic-terrorism/

Tesi v. The State of Texas. (2014). 02–12-00096-CR. *Court of Appeals 297th District Court of Tarrant County*.

United States Department of Justice. (2019, June 7). *Defendant found guilty for making false statements in Garland shooting investigation*. [Press release]. Retrieved from https://www.justice.gov/usao-az/pr/defendant-found-guilty-making-false-statements-garland-shooting-investigation

WMAZ. (2018, December 14). Convicted cult leader Malachi York files $2 billion lawsuit. *13WMAZ.com*. Retrieved from https://www.13wmaz.com/article/news/local/convicted-cult-leader-malachi-york-files-2-billion-lawsuit/93-623499810

Chapter 6
Sovereign Citizens in Court

Chapter six explores the behavior of sovereign citizens in court. Many defendants, who claim to be sovereign citizens, refuse to participate in the legal proceedings and or espouse unusual beliefs that may appear to be delusional in nature. Research about mental health and competency issues will be reviewed. Court records are used to elucidate and identify, some of the more common courtroom tactics used by sovereign citizens.

Sovereign citizens are known for their problematic behavior in court. They can be obstinate, argumentative, antagonistic, confrontational, and disruptive. They tend to file lengthy, nonsensical motions, sometimes hundreds of pages in length. They attempt to present written notices trying to prove that the court is acting fraudulently, arguing that state and federal courts are actually admiralty courts (Parker 2014). Proof of this, they say, are the golden-fringed flags hanging in U.S. courtrooms. They often refuse to follow orders, disobey courtroom rules, some to the point of having to be removed from the premises, held in contempt of court or barred from attendance in court altogether. They will improperly object to motions, ask inappropriate questions, repeat the phrase "Let the record show…" in an effort to ensure that every aspect of the court procedure is recorded, question the authority of the court, and read long lists of Supreme Court decisions they believe bolsters their argument. A common tactic is requesting that the court "prove" jurisdiction and demanding that the judge "prove" their oath of office.

Some sovereign citizens will refuse to answer any questions or even be sworn in. When asked their name they will not respond or indicate that they do not understand. Some may claim that they are there by "special appearance" and are in the courtroom "under duress." Refusal to enter a plea is common, which forces the judge to enter a plea on their behalf. They often insist on representing themselves

---

The original version of this chapter was revised. The correction to this chapter is available at https://doi.org/10.1007/978-3-030-45851-5_8

© The Author(s), under exclusive license to Springer Nature Switzerland AG 2020, Corrected Publication 2020
C. M. Sarteschi, *Sovereign Citizens*, SpringerBriefs in Psychology, https://doi.org/10.1007/978-3-030-45851-5_6

(pro se), rejecting court appointed attorneys, (i.e. "you can't force a lawyer on me") or any assistance from the court, and fire their own counsel. Many will attempt to film the courtroom procedures, arguing that they have a right to do so. When told by the judge that they are not allowed to film, they have been known to continue doing so anyway, by placing the camera in a secret location.

Certain cases are particularly illustrative. Hamond Mormon, a Moorish sovereign citizen, was convicted of armed robbery, aggravated assault, kidnapping, false imprisonment, among other charges, and was sentenced to 55 years in prison. During his trial, he defended himself and filed a number of motions indicating that he was a "true flesh-and-blood American and sovereign citizen" refusing to participate "in colorable law schemes or practices." At one point during his trial, he refused to wear clothing and instead wore a blanket. He eventually decided not to enter the courtroom altogether. Despite his refusal to wear clothing, an extensive mental status evaluation deemed him competent to stand trial (Kissel 2019).

In another noteworthy instance, a Moorish sovereign citizen couple, identified as John and Jane Doe in court documents, were arrested after squatting in a home. The criminal charges stemmed from the couple allowing their daughter to live in a home that was deemed "unfit for human habitation." The couple refused to participate in any aspect of the legal process because of their belief that the court lacked proper jurisdiction (Beauge 2019). John Doe walked out of courtroom after objecting to a "kangaroo court." They continually and loudly interrupted the prosecutor during opening statements, shouting out phrases such as "there is no justice here" and claiming to have been unlawfully imprisoned (Beauge 2019). Despite their nonparticipation in the trial, a jury found them guilty in "abstentia" of four misdemeanor counts of endangering the welfare of a child, resisting arrest, causing a public nuisance, and disorderly conduct (Strawser 2016). They were sentenced to serve up to 11 years in prison (Beauge 2019).

A sovereign citizen with a lengthy rap sheet, who, in court records is referred to as a "repeat felony offender," ("RFEL"), had most recently been arrested for burglary, criminal trespassing, and a number of other charges. He decided to plead guilty to one charge instead of taking his chances with a jury trial. On the day of his sentencing, he arrived in court but absconded because he did not like what he heard in the courtroom. A bench warrant was issued. He was apprehended a year later in New Mexico.

While awaiting extradition to Pennsylvania, the detention center in which he was being held started receiving a series of faxes from a "Continental United States Superior Court Judge." The warden indicated that he thought the document looked "pretty decent." A second fax arrived naming the individuals who were on their way to the jail to retrieve the sovereign citizen in question. The warden contacted a local marshal who attempted to determine if the release request was legitimate. They learned that the "court," attempting to release the sovereign citizen, was themselves a group of sovereign citizens, one of whom was the wife of the absconder. Eventually, two men and two women arrived at the jail, complete with official-looking badges, armed with guns and a knife. Jail officials, who were now aware of the scam, quickly took them into custody. Those involved were surprised at the boldness of the illegal behavior. They were so bold in their actions precisely because they did not believe they were doing anything illegal. The warden explained that "they fully feel their sovereignty gives them rightful authority and they are legitimate law enforcement" (Dendinger 2017, para. 26).

The boldness continued. That same absconding sovereign citizen subsequently filed a federal lawsuit against the judge involved in his burglary case, along with other court officials for allegedly "coercing" him into pleading guilty (Strawser 2016). The goal of the lawsuit was to withdraw his guilty plea. He claimed that they were "threatening to take [his] bail away if [he] did not plead guilty" which he claimed "violates [his] rights." The lawsuit alleged a litany of typical sovereign citizen claims, including that the court in which he pled guilty was not a real court but rather a "business for profit." The lawsuit went on to claim that the court was a "admiralty maritime Court, as you can tell the gold fringed black (sic). We haven't had a judge since 1776, we have Court Administrators." "I'm not a US citizen, I'm a non-citizen national… I'm under God's law, I'm under the common law… I'm not a citizen to a government but we have a right to declare nationality as part of the universal declaration of human rights signed on by Obama through United Nations." His withdrawal request was denied. (*Commonwealth of Pennsylvania. v. Pankotai* 2017).

In another case, "a live man," was sentenced to 51 months imprisonment and three years of supervised release for tax evasion. Upon his release from prison, he filed multiple motions regarding his desire to abate restitution, to recuse the judge from further proceedings and requested permission to associate with other felons while on supervised release. The heart of his complaint involved "purported agents" of the U.S. Treasury Department, the U.S. Attorney General's office, the Bureau of Prisons as well as the director of a Virginia halfway house who he claims conspired to deprive him of his constitutional rights and who successfully stole "15 years of his life, liberty and production," which cost him approximately $50 million. Among other requests, he asked the court to "acknowledge the dissolution" of himself as a "jurist person" as well as impanel a jury under the "civilian flag" of the U.S. Ultimately, the court recognized that his arguments were without merit and based on sovereign citizen ideology (*West v. Purported Agents of Sec'y* 2019).

A sovereign citizen who considers himself a "State National of the Republic" and calls himself "Christopher The Living Man" caused a major disruption in a South Dakota courtroom after being arrested for stalking a local mayor (Sneve 2019). He is also accused of making statements about having the prosecutor killed, leaving the country, and about the judge "going down" (Jorgensen 2019). He filed a federal lawsuit against the mayor he is accused of stalking filled with a host of frivolous claims. During his first court appearance for the stalking charges, he was very disruptive. He continued to talk over the judge and prosecutor. At one point, he swore at the judge. In previous court appearances, he has claimed that the court does not have jurisdiction over him, that he does not "consent" to the proceedings or understand the charges against him (Jorgensen 2019). He has a history of harassing local government employees and has served prison time for disorderly conduct and filing a false police report (Weill 2019).

That same sovereign citizen was known for attending Sioux Falls City Council meetings and causing problems. One of his main complaints involved 5G phone service. He is "blowing the whistle" on 5G service, due to his belief in a conspiracy theory that it poses a danger to the public and it is a scheme involving shadowy governments attempting to deprive people of their liberty (Sneve 2019). His maintains a blog where he writes about (among other things) his belief that the U.S. is a corporation owned by the Queen of England and that laws do not apply to him (Weill 2019). He considers himself a freedom fighter who is risking his life to blog (Weill 2019). One of his more recent blog posts about 5G service included a picture of the first 5G "death tower" to appear in Sioux Falls. He asks the question: "how is this not "purposeful genocide?" His blog is replete with sovereign citizen ideology and other conspiratorial laden ideas including, but not limited to: that one's birth certificate is "immediately monetized, is worth millions, and is traded on the stock market"; "The Law", Rules, Codes, Ordinances and Statutes are NOT REAL LAW"; you do not need a driver's license, per THE UNIFORM COMMERCIAL CODE ITSELF"; the U.S. DOLLAR is worth nothing; "modern medicine…[is] there to KEEP YOU SICK"; fluoride that's put in your water supply is not naturally occurring… IT'S AN INDUSTRIAL POISON MEANT TO KEEP THE POPULATION DRUGGED." As of this writing, his felony stalking charges have yet to be adjudicated.

6.1 Sovereign Citizens and Mental Illness

It is common for judges unfamiliar with sovereign citizen ideology to send defendants espousing such rhetoric for mental health status evaluations. Their behavior in court is often unusual, atypical, and as Mark Pitcavage (2011) noted in his research on this subject, often devolves into a "strange territory." It can be difficult to fathom why sovereign citizens repeatedly engage in behavior that goes against their own best interests and that never results in a positive outcome. "They must be crazy" is a common sentiment when considering the behavior of the sovereign citizen. After all, sane, psychologically healthy people do not purposefully engage in behavior that would cause themselves more trouble. However, that is precisely what sovereign citizens do. They engage in behavior and tactics that harm their chances of winning their case. They believe in ideas without objective evidence and ignore the fact, that there exists a great deal of evidence contradicting their beliefs. Even in the face of available evidence, in virtually every case, sovereign citizens continue to act in accordance with their own beliefs. Therefore, it is no surprise that many observers question whether sovereign citizens are mentally ill.

6.2 Review of the Literature

Despite their evidently bizarre behavior and outrageous claims, and the sovereign citizen's willingness to engage in tactics that have no chance of succeeding, the majority do not have a diagnosable mental illness. There is no identifiable mental condition or disorder that explains the behavior or beliefs of sovereign citizens. Perhaps the two closest are schizotypal, a condition which encompasses personality traits such suspiciousness and magical thinking, and that is correlated with belief in conspiracy theories (Pierre 2019), and delusional disorder, the latter of which is classified as a psychotic disorder. Mental health professionals who perform court-ordered competency evaluations, likewise often find that the beliefs of sovereign citizens do not meet the diagnostic criteria for any specific psychiatric condition. To date, very little empirical literature exists about sovereign citizens in general. What is available regarding their mental health is even more limited.

Pytyck and Chaimowitz (2013) conducted case studies on two sovereign citizens, referred by the court, for assessment of their fitness to stand trial. The first sovereign citizen was a 47-year-old male who failed to appear in court. He had been arrested while asleep at the wheel of an idling car and refusing a breathalyzer. He also refused to identify himself to the officers and was uncooperative with the judge. He argued that the court had no jurisdiction over him and that his birth certificate served as key evidence in his case. Upon his assessment, he was diagnosed as having a psychotic disorder, likely a delusional disorder. He had previously participated in outpatient therapy for paranoid ideation associated with workplace occurrences. After his mental fitness evaluation, he underwent inpatient treatment and was given antipsychotic medication which had minimal impact on his sovereign citizen belief system. He was described by the ward staff as being confident, entitled, grandiose, and narcissistic. In addition to his sovereign citizen ideology, he held other conspiratorial ideas involving numerology, homeopathic and natural medicine. While never abandoning his sovereign citizen legal theories during inpatient treatment, he did eventually become more willing to cooperate and admitted that his refusal to participate was entirely on purpose. The evaluators eventually determined that he could understand the court proceedings. He was returned to court and released on bail.

The second sovereign citizen case involved a 50-year-old woman with no previous criminal record or psychiatric history. She had been arrested after failing to comply with the authorities during a traffic stop in which she lacked the proper vehicle registration, driver's license and insurance. She refused to identify herself, indicating that she was not required to because of common law, resisted arrest and upon detainment, declined to be searched. Upon evaluation to stand trial, she continued to refuse to cooperate, though she did share with the evaluators some of her sovereign citizen beliefs including the importance of birth certificates, and her right to opt out of the laws of society. It was ultimately determined that she was fit to stand trial and did not receive a mental health diagnosis, (at least not one that was revealed in their report). Based on the review of these two cases, the authors contend that, in their estimation, the majority of sovereign citizens are neither psychotic nor unfit to stand trial (Pytyck and Chaimowitz 2013).

A similar finding was made by Parker in his 2014 study of nine sovereign citizens between 2001 and 2012. The average age of his sample was approximately 39 years old. The majority were reasonably well-educated, African American males. None had a history of psychosis and most appeared to have a relatively normal upbringing. Six of the nine agreed to undergo an in-person mental status examination. Of those, none demonstrated significant cognitive deficits. One was diagnosed with delusional disorder and was deemed incompetent to stand trial; one had recurrent depression; three had substance abuse disorders; and one had no psychiatric diagnosis. Upon further reflection, Parker (2014) came to believe that the sovereign citizen defendant who had been diagnosed with a delusional disorder did not truly meet the criteria for the diagnosis and was "almost certainly" competent to stand trial (p. 347). He argued that those who adhere to sovereign citizen beliefs are not psychotic but are best understood as holding an extremist political philosophy. Although sovereign citizens can vary in their beliefs, they generally adhere to a shared or common belief system. Parker (2014) argues that this shared belief system *alone* does not warrant a mental health diagnosis or a judgement of incompetence to stand trial.

In a 2018 study by Paradis, Owen, and McCullough, they conducted a retrospective review of 36 criminal cases of sovereign citizens who had undergone competency-to-stand trial evaluations (CST) between 2007 and 2016 in Kings County, New York. The researchers scanned approximately 2000 archived computer files to locate their cases. Of the 36 sovereign citizen cases included in the sample, all were male, mostly African American, and their average age was 38.7. The majority had graduated high school or had a GED, and were born in the U.S.; 17% were immigrants. Six of the 36 individuals in the study were thought to have been Moors or Muurs, and may have been members of the Moorish church or a related organization. At least one sovereign citizen in their study was Hispanic. Like other studies assessing the mental health of sovereign citizens, the majority were deemed competent and not psychotic.

To date, all of the available published studies about the mental health of sovereign citizens have indicated that the majority are not psychotic nor unfit to stand trial. Even in cases when a sovereign citizen was diagnosed with a psychotic disorder, researchers were skeptical about the accuracy of those diagnoses. Judges familiar with the tactics of sovereign citizens seem to be referring fewer sovereign citizens for competency evaluations, at least that was the case for Parker (2018) who indicated that since 2012, he has experienced a reduction of sovereign citizens being referred for competency evaluations. He attributes the reduction to an increased awareness among judges who recognize that sovereign citizen beliefs alone do not constitute evidence of a mental disorder or an inability to comprehend court procedures (Parker 2018). It is unknown whether judges, more broadly, also share that same level of awareness and are also referring fewer cases for competency evaluations.

6.3 Female Sovereign Citizens

One observation made by several researchers, in the aforementioned studies, is the lack of females in their sample. Paradis et al. (2018) theorized that may be because females comprise a smaller percentage of the justice system population. They also theorized that females may be less likely to utilize sovereign citizen tactics in court because as primary caretakers of children, they are less willing to risk the possibility of additional legal sanctions that could be imposed upon them should they lose.

As they noted in their study, some females do attempt to utilize sovereign citizen court tactics. One such case is that of Heather Ann Tucci-Jarraf, a sovereign citizen recently convicted of conspiracy to commit money laundering in 2018 and sentenced to five years in prison. She had been acting as an unlicensed attorney for Randall Beane. They both had engaged in an effort to defraud a bank of more than $31 million. During their joint jury trial, she represented herself (as did her codefendant) and asserted a number of sovereign citizen ideas including that the government, a federal corporation, in her view, had been foreclosed upon and had no jurisdiction over her, and that the U.S. hides secret accounts for individuals in the Federal Reserve Bank (i.e. the straw man theory) (United States Department of Justice 2018). She was also known to file voluminous rambling nonsensical legal documents, another common tactic of sovereign citizens.

The judge described her as being difficult, starting with the swearing-in process, when she refused to say "I do" instead repeating the phrase "I am the source of all that is." The judge responded that he did not ask her what her source was and encouraged her to affirm that she will tell the truth. She responded that "I just said I swear to speak true, accurate and complete" and when pressed further argued that "truth is a matter of perception, whereas speaking true, accurate, and complete gives you a full accurate record." As the trial proceeded, the defendant continued to argue with many of the questions the judge was asking, answering in ways that were seemingly nonsensical but in line with sovereign citizen ideology. She also adamantly insisted on representing herself, another common choice made by sovereign citizens, in court. Her argument to defend herself involved her claim of having represented herself in criminal court in the past and having practiced law for 17 years, though for 11 of the 17 years, she "was a barred attorney" after she "cancelled" her license in 2011 (*United States of America v. Tucci-Jarraf* 2017).

After her conviction, Ms. Tucci-Jarraf appealed her case, as did her co-conspirator Mr. Beane. In September 2019, an appellate court affirmed the earlier rulings, rejecting their appeals. The crux of their appeal was that because of their unusual beliefs-- their sovereign citizen ideology, they should have been forced to accept legal counsel. In the appellate opinion, the court addressed the matter by answering two main questions: (1) did the defendants waive the right to counsel in a knowing and intelligent manner; and (2) were the defendants mentally competent to serve their own lawyers?

Regarding the first question, the court observed that each defendant was granted the appropriate vetting process to determine if they were able to represent themselves. The court warned them of the dangers inherent in representing themselves and they remained "unequivocal" in their wish to proceed with self-representation. Both defendants, the court observed, requested standby counsel, unprompted by the judge. The court also notes the fact that both defendants had previously worked high-level, demanding jobs; Mr. Beane, as an electrical engineer and Ms. Tucci-Jarraf, as a prosecutor and public defender. Both had previously defended themselves in court on other matters. The criminal conduct, of which they had been convicted, involved "complex financial activity... demonstrating plenty of mental acuity." It is also important to note that neither defendant had a documented history of psychological problems. The court indicated that both defendants were able to understand the roles of the court, interact with court personnel in a courteous manner, collaborate with their appointed standby counsel, and raise relatively few minor objections during trial. Though they espoused "impossible conspiracy theories" they were still able to effectively cross-examine witnesses, offer contextual biographical narratives during testimony, and clearly articulate how their sovereign citizen belief systems led them to commit financial crimes. Thus, the evidence strongly supports the notion that the defendants waived the right to counsel in a knowing and intelligent manner.

Regarding the second question about self-representation, the court observes that having unconventional and conspiracy-oriented beliefs alone does not establish proof of an unsound mind. The Supreme Court, the court noted, has never indicated that eccentric worldviews by themselves are evidence of mental incompetence. "The hard fact is that intelligent people, even very intelligent people, can believe baffling things. The same brain that allows them to be very intelligent, can when combined with financial and other stresses, trigger all kinds of irrational behavior... Count also the thousands of other straw man conspiracy theory proponents nationwide. These individuals of course are misguided, some dangerously so. But that doesn't mean they inhabit a "private mental world" wholly divorced from reality. And it certainly doesn't shield them from the consequences of their actions." The court's opinion regarding the mental competency of Mr. Beane and Ms. Tucci-Jarraf is consistent with existing research about sovereign citizen ideology. Irrational, eccentric, sovereign citizen beliefs, by themselves, are not proof of mental illness. (*United States of America v Tucci-Jarraf; Beane* 2019).

In another case involving a female Ohio sovereign citizen charged with multiple counts of "Dog at Large," Donna Farley appeared for trial and argued that certain UCC resolutions indicated that the court had no jurisdiction over her. She was ultimately found guilty of the charges. On appeal, she acted as her own attorney and again argued that the court had no jurisdiction over her. In a five-page document filed with the court, entitled "Courtesy Notice," which the court indicated was a product of the "The One People's Public Trust," she argued that she "never gave her consent to be governed" and that such a document provided the trial court with information of "the new legal, lawful and unrebutted landscape ushered in last year with the UCC filings." The court recognized these filings as being "sovereign citizen" in nature and found no merit in her arguments (*State v. Farley* 2013). Coincidentally, "The One People's Public Trust" was a group originally founded by the aforementioned Ms.Tucci-Jarraf (Hatewatch Staff 2017).

In another instance, a female sovereign citizen defendant, indicted on felony child abuse and neglect charges, filed a "Notice of Removal" in an effort to move her state criminal case to federal court. She also claimed that the state had no jurisdiction over her, citing as authority the 1931 Statue of Westminster, the Articles of Confederation, the Treaty of Ghent and the 1836 Treaty of Marrakesh. She also took issue with the registration of her birth, indicating that it was "a contract between

[her] mother and the U.S. Government Corporation[,] who did not tell her [mother] that she was selling [defendant], a flesh and blood child, to the state...Corporation as a the Chattel Property/Slave, which is a violation of Human Rights." A review of court documents indicates that she also "cc'd" the Pope and the state governor. (*Missouri v. Haley* 2019).

In what began as a routine traffic stop, a member of the "American National People's Creator" ("a nonresident private organization") argued with police that she had the constitutional right to travel freely, did not need to register her car and had canceled her driver's license. It was her belief that she was not bound to any other law other than God's law. She was arrested and her car was impounded. Later that day, she was hit by a car while crossing the street. It never would have occurred, she argued, had they not taken away her car. She subsequently filed a series of complaints against all parties involved in a case, including the state governor, and the Secretary of State. Her complaint outlined 14 different claims against the defendants including: false arrest, unlawful imprisonment, violating her alleged right to travel by "refusing to dismiss" her case because of their desire to commercially profit from cases like hers, violating the seventh amendment by "not settling claim for injury at common law and moving martial law/martial law equity under the color of law," and violating her 13th amendment rights by intending to make her a slave." Recognizing her claims as being consistent with the sovereign citizen movement, and thus invalid, her case was dismissed (*Yun v. New Jersey* 2019).

Cherron Phillips (AKA "River Tali El Bey") is a sovereign citizen whose behavior in court was especially problematic. Her disruptions first became apparent during her younger brothers' trial for trafficking cocaine. She filed a number of pseudo legal documents objecting to the court's jurisdiction over her brother's case, arguing that he was not subject to US laws (Ortega 2014). In one motion, she asked for the case against her alter ego to be dismissed and regarded her criminal case as a civil matter (Ortega 2014). She was known to give speeches in court, bring crowds of people and to advise her brother on how to respond to questions (Ortega 2014). Her behavior was so disruptive that she was eventually barred from the courthouse (Meisner 2014). Her brother was found guilty.

In the summer of 2011 and after his sentencing, it was discovered that in the spring of 2011, Ms. Phillips had filed maritime liens in excess of $100 billion against the property of 12 public officials involved in her brother's court case. These actions led to her arrest and prosecution. During her trial, should would not allow a lawyer to represent her, refused to file a plea and would respond to questions regarding a plea with "I accept for value and return for value for settlement and closure of this matter" (Dey 2017). Her sovereign citizen tactics were unsuccessful. She was sentenced to seven years in federal prison, six months longer than was recommended by prosecutors. The judge involved in her case, called her a "paper terrorist," and noted that even before her trial had begun, she would send him letters naming him and the prosecutor as defendants in a lawsuit filed in Washington (Meisner 2014).

Since her conviction, she continues to file motions from prison. In 2015, she argued that she is "imprisoned without authority in violation of civil rights promised by the United States…" That action was dismissed. In 2017, she tried to convince the judge that she should be released on the grounds that Congress had failed to publish the federal law she violated with the Federal Register. The judge responded by indicating that her argument was "easily disposed of" because "Congress is not required to publish criminal statutes in the Federal Register" (Dey 2017). Court records from July 2019 indicate that she has twice attempted to remove the court's 2011 order restricting her filings and access to the courthouse. She argues that the restriction order is invalid and that her due process rights were violated. The court again rejected these motions and this time added a warning that she is to stop raising these arguments that have already been decided against her. Prison does not seem to have much deterred her from filing frivolous motions.

Ms. Phillips appears to be from a family of sovereign citizens. Her brother represented himself and filed a number of typical sovereign citizen motions during his trial. Her parents were indicted on federal tax evasion charges. Like many sovereign citizens, they too chose self-representation during their trials. They were convicted on conspiracy charges to defraud the government and both sentenced to 41 months in prison (Ortega 2014).

In court, sovereign citizens often insist on self-representation, spar with attorneys and judges, file many lengthy, pseudolegal motions, are disruptive, and are often unwilling to participate in the normal criminal justice process. Some refuse to enter a plea or even appear for court, forcing the court to move forward in their absence. Even after having been convicted of a crime, some will continue to file motions, and attempt to disrupt the traditional legal process. While the majority of sovereign citizens are males, there are females who espouse sovereign citizen ideology and who adopt similar tactics in court. Such behavior at times can appear strikingly odd and bizarre giving the illusion of mental illness but studies and court rulings consistently show that the majority of sovereign citizens are not mentally ill and are competent to stand trial. Thus far, there appears to be no link between mental illness and sovereign citizens.

References

Beauge, J. (2019, March 8). Two 'sovereign citizens' refused to recognize the court's authority—and still got convicted. Patriot news. Retrieved from https://www.pennlive.com/crime/2019/05/two-sovereign-citizens-refused-to-recognize-the-courts-authority-and-still-got-convicted.html

Commonwealth of Pennsylvania. v. Pankotai. 903 MDA. (2017). *Supreme Court of Pennsylvania*. 2017.

Dendinger, J. M. (2017, February 10). Attempted jailbreak: Four taken into custody; claim sovereignty. *News-Bulletin*. Retrieved fromhttp://www.news-bulletin.com/news/attempted-jail-break/article_ac8c9b0a-ee40-11e6-8d69-473a1484a591.html

Dey, J. (2017, August 29): Strange characters make for strange cases. *The News-Gazette*. Retrieved from https://www.news-gazette.com/news/jim-dey-strange-characters-make-for-strange-cases/article_aff06299-a5e0-54aa-9808-1ad6a6473bef.html

Hatewatch Staff. (2017). The Sovereign Files: 8.15.2017. *The Southern Poverty Law Center*. Retrieved from https://www.splcenter.org/hatewatch/2017/08/15/sovereign-files-8152017

Jorgenen, D. (2019, June 13). Stalking suspect swears at judge. *Keloland Media Group*. Retrieved from https://www.keloland.com/news/local-news/stalking-suspect-swears-at-judge/

Kissel, N. (2019, March 11). Bizarre trial ends with 55 year sentence for armed robber. *FYNTV*. Retrieved from https://fannin.fetchyournews.com/2019/03/11/bizarre-trial-ends-with-55-year-sentence-for-armed-robber/

Meisner, J. (2014, October 14). "Sovereign citizen" given 7 years in prison. *Chicago Tribune*. Retrieved from https://www.chicagotribune.com/news/ct-sovereign-citizen-sentencing-met-20141014-story.html

Missouri v. Haley. (2019). 4:19-cv-02303-JMB. *United States District Court for the Eastern District of Missouri, Eastern Division.*

Ortega, T. (2014, August 26). Cherron Phillips: Chicago's sovereign citizen 'paper terrorist' and her NBA secret. *Cult Education Institute*. Retrieved from https://culteducation.com/group/1142-sovereign-citizen-movement/27722-cherron-phillips-chicago-s-sovereign-citize-paper-terrorist-and-her-nba-secret.html

Paradis, C. M., Owen, E., & McCullough, G. (2018). Evaluations of urban sovereign citizens' competency to stand trial. *The Journal of the American Academy of Psychiatry and the Law, 46*(2), 158–166. https://doi.org/10.29158/JAAPL.003758-18.

Parker, G. F. (2014). Competence to stand trial evaluations of sovereign citizens: A case series and primer of odd political and legal beliefs. *The Journal of the American Academy of Psychiatry and the Law, 42*(3), 338–349. Retrieved from http://jaapl.org/content/42/3/338.

Parker, G. F. (2018). Sovereign citizens and competency to stand trial. *The Journal of the American Academy of Psychiatry and the Law, 46*(2), 4. https://doi.org/10.29158/JAAPL.003743-18.

Pierre, J. M. (2019). Integrating Non-psychiatric models of delusion-like beliefs into forensic psychiatric assessment. *The Journal of the American Academy of Psychiatry and the Law, 47*(2), 1–9. https://doi.org/10.29158/JAAPL.003833-19.

Pitcavage, M. (2011). Strange territory: Ideology and incompetency in the courtroom. *Anti-Defamation League*. Retrieved from https://www.scribd.com/document/54785226/Strange-Territory-2011.

Pytyck, J., & Chaimowitz, G. A. (2013). The sovereign citizen movement and fitness to stand trial. *International Journal of Forensic Mental Health, 12*(2), 149–153. https://doi.org/10.1080/14999013.2013.796329.

Sneve, Joe. (2019, June 14). Christopher 'The Living Man' Bruce has history of clashing with public officials. *Argus Leader*. Retrieved from https://www.argusleader.com/story/news/2019/06/14/christopher-the-living-man-bruce-has-history-clashing-public-officials/1448694001/

State v. Farley. (2013). 2013-Ohio-5517. *Ohio Court of Appeals.*

Strawser, J. (2016, January 26). Mount caramel man Faust federal lawsuit against judge, attorneys. *The Daily Item*. Retrieved from https://www.dailyitem.com/news/mount-carmel-man-files-federal-lawsuit-against-judge-attorneys/article_43f3841c-c48b-11e5-96b5-03337d535895.html

United States Department of Justice. (2018, February 1). *Federal jury convicts Knoxville man and former Washington state prosecutor turned leader of sovereign citizen movement of wire fraud and conspiracy to commit money laundering*. [Press release]. Retrieved from https://www.justice.gov/usao-edtn/pr/federal-jury-convicts-knoxville-man-and-former-washington-state-prosecutor-turned

United States of America v Tucci-Jarraf. (2017). 3:17-CR-82. *United States District Court for the Eastern District of Tennessee at Knoxville.*

United States of America v Tucci-Jarraf; Beane. (2019). 3:17-cr-00082. *United States Court of Appeals For The Sixth Circuit.*

Weill, K. (2019, June 18). Sovereign citizen tells judge 'fuck you' after allegedly stalking Mayor over 5G conspiracy theory. *The Daily Beast*. Retrieved from https://www.thedailybeast.com/sovereign-citizen-tells-judge-fuck-you-after-allegedly-stalking-mayor-over-5g-conspiracy-theory

West v. Purported Agents of Sec'y. (2019). 1:19:cv-00107-MR-WCM. *United States Court for the Western District of North Carolina, Asheville Division.*

Yun v. New Jersey. (2019). 18.cv-1804 (KM) (SCM). *United States Court for the District of New Jersey.*

Chapter 7
Countering the Sovereign Citizen Movement

Chapter seven describes needed efforts for preventing or countermanding the most prevalent tactics of sovereign citizens. It discusses some of the challenges associated with deterring the movement. It also proposes changes in policy and law to effectively address the problem of the sovereign citizen movement.

7.1 Laws

Harsher penalties are needed to combat the damage done by sovereign citizens. We know from previous chapters that individual states have strengthened their laws against the fraudulent filings of sovereign citizens. Many states have yet to address this problem and the wrongdoings of sovereign citizens resulting in only civil penalties. Civil penalties are the sanctions most commonly used against sovereign citizens in the fight against their paper terrorism (Weir 2015). Civil penalties are not enough. Civil sanctions and penalties, simply are too weak to act as a sufficient deterrent. Criminal sanctions and penalties must be put in place to more effectively deter their fraudulent behavior.

Missouri recently passed HB 1769 which establishes the offense of the false filing of legal documents. What is notable about this particular law is that once an agency becomes aware of a suspicious filing or record, they are required to notify law enforcement (House Bill N0.1769 2018). Nevada has recently proposed a bill to combat the ever-increasing problem that sovereign citizens represent to their state. Assembly Bill 15 would make it a felony to create fake judgments, summons, complaints, and most other court documents (Lockhead 2019). If convicted, an offender could face up to four years in prison (Lockhead 2019).

The original version of this chapter was revised. The correction to this chapter is available at https://doi.org/10.1007/978-3-030-45851-5_8

© The Author(s), under exclusive license to Springer Nature Switzerland AG 2020, Corrected Publication 2020
C. M. Sarteschi, *Sovereign Citizens*, SpringerBriefs in Psychology, https://doi.org/10.1007/978-3-030-45851-5_7

Florida is a state with tougher penalties. A sovereign citizen was recently sentenced to 40 years in prison for mailing various court officials fraudulent, supposed legal documents which claimed that the state owed him tens of millions of dollars (Stockler 2019). Mr. Rosado, wrote in one court filing, "I am a PRIVATE Citizen of the Florida Republic Union state and… have not waived any of my constitutionally protected YAHWEH (G-D) GIVEN rights secured under the national and state constitutions of this country." He also identified himself as being a member of a law firm called the Reichmann Group, which, on its website claims not to be a "public law firm or a member of any state's private Bar Association" (Stockler 2019). His 40-year sentence sets the right precedent to be followed by other states looking to deter paper terrorism.

In many states, it remains far too easy to file fraudulent liens. Anyone can file a lien, even from behind prison walls. Many states are reactionary in their efforts to change their lien laws. For instance, Tennessee officials, including the county mayor, city police officers, county deputies, state troopers, and other officials at all levels of government, were hit with fraudulent liens totaling more than $2 billion (Lakin 2017). State officials are now attempting to pass a law to make it easier to fight fraudulent liens but a much better step would be to make it exceedingly difficult to file fraudulent liens, in the first place.

7.2 Squatting and Traffic Stops

State laws are also ill-equipped to prevent sovereign citizens and other individuals from squatting in homes. Squatting is particularly prevalent among some Moorish sovereign citizens who feel that they have special ownership of certain lands because of their alleged indigenous roots. Sovereign citizens often take squatting a step further and attempt to become landlords of the property, illegally renting it out to others. Mark Pitcavage of the Anti-Defamation League (ADL), notes that the two most common types of violence associated with sovereign citizens involve traffic stops and residence visits (visits to the squatter's residence) (Whitmire 2015). Forced evictions can quickly turn violent. These are some of the most dangerous calls for law enforcement officials.

As described previously, police are often unable to effectively intervene in squatting situations. Sovereign citizens produce pseudolegal paperwork claiming ownership of the property. It is not the job of the law enforcement officer to make a determination of the legality of sovereign citizen paperwork. In one recent situation, an armed sovereign citizen refused to leave a rental property. Police temporarily detained the man and determined that he currently had arrest warrants in another state. However, "law enforcement agencies did not have a desire to extradite him" and subsequently released him (Givens and King 2019). In cases where sovereign citizens are arrested, it is not uncommon for them to return to the home in which they have been squatting the very next day. There is no national data tracking the number of sovereign citizen squatters or problematic police interactions occurring with squatting sovereign citizens. More effective remedies are needed to combat this ongoing problem.

In most states, squatting is considered a civil issue, not a criminal issue, and this severely limits the ability of law enforcement to intervene in a squatting situation. Squatting, is when one person or multiple persons move into a property, which they have absolutely no legal right to, nor ownership of and take up residence. This should be a black and white issue. One would expect that if they were to come home and find a burglar living in their basement, the police would quickly solve their problem. However, burglary is a crime and squatting is a civil offense. When a homeowner returns to their vacation home or a vacant rental property or their empty house which has been on the market for six months and finds someone or a family of someone's living in their home, most often calling the police will accomplish absolutely nothing. Thousands of dollars in legal costs, multiple trips to the courtroom and the passage of many months, must occur before the squatter can be removed by the police. Shouldn't all laws be changed such that squatting is a criminal offense so that squatters will be quickly removed and arrested by the police? This is not a gray area. Either you own the car or you do not. If you do not own the vehicle nor have you been given the right by the owner of the vehicle, to drive the vehicle, then driving the vehicle should result in your arrest. If you do not own said home but you are living in that un-owned home, never having been given the right to do so by the owner of the home, should you not be arrested for living there? Unfortunately, in most states, it remains a civil issue and the police are largely powerless to remove the squatters from your home.

Some of the deadliest encounters for police have started with routine traffic stops. One survey of 20 police agencies recently found that traffic-related offenses accounted for nearly all contacts police had with sovereign citizens (Smith 2019). Sovereign citizens, some of whom are known to be extensively armed (Hate Crimes & The Threat of Domestic Terrorism 2012), frequently come in the contact with police because of their refusal to follow basic traffic laws. It is not uncommon for them to drive unlicensed, or with currently suspended licenses, in unregistered vehicles with no plates, or displaying self-made plates. Once pulled over, the sovereign citizen refuses to follow even the most basic commands from law enforcement, often forcing a confrontation. Despite these sometimes deadly encounters, there still exists no standardized training programs concerning sovereign citizens (Smith 2019). It is imperative that criminal justice professionals across the spectrum, are educated about the dangers of sovereign citizens. An aptly titled article about the movement sums it up perfectly: "What you don't know about sovereign citizens can hurt you" (Smith 2019).

There exists no national data regarding training programs for the sovereign citizen movement. One analyst revealed in his 2012 congressional testimony that the Justice Department's Bureau of Justice Assistance (BJA) makes available training to state and local law enforcement about the sovereign citizen threat (Hate Crimes & The Threat of Domestic Terrorism 2012). That program began in 2010, however, it is unclear if it still exists.

Detectives Kory Flowers and Rob Finch of the North Carolina Police Intelligence Squad developed their own program, in response to the many problems they were having with sovereign citizens. They train all members of the criminal justice system about the sovereign citizen threat including dispatchers, the register of deeds, the clerk of courts, district and Superior Court judges, assistant district attorneys, defense attorneys, parking enforcement officers, meter reading professionals, and even fire inspectors, and fire department building inspectors. The detectives have observed that the more information each law enforcement individual possesses about sovereign citizens, the more prepared they are to do their job safely and effectively (Beirich 2012). The training program described by Flowers and Finch should be available across all states and expanded to include private citizens, because they too have been victims of paper terrorism and violence. Education about the basic issues and problems associated with sovereign citizens, could prevent further victimization.

7.3 The Courts

Sovereign citizens are a major problem in the courtroom yet courts are reluctant to impose sanctions on them (McRoberts 2019). This may in part stem from a lack of awareness regarding the tools that are at their disposal. March-Safbom (2018) reported that more than half of the respondents in her survey of court professionals were unaware of the measures taken by their respective states to combat sovereign citizens. This lack of awareness may embolden sovereign citizens to create havoc in the courtroom.

The fight to reduce sovereign citizen misbehavior in the courtroom is ongoing. However, Parker (2014) learned from his conference interactions with judges that because these cases are time-consuming, prosecutors are sometimes apt to dismiss a case against them in order to avoid wasting resources. Additionally, he found judges who had more direct experience with sovereign citizens, referred fewer of them for psychological evaluations, than did those who had less experience (Parker 2014). This would suggest that familiarity with sovereign citizens may lead to less tolerance of their antics.

Judges and other court personnel, who are unfamiliar with sovereign citizens, often have the most trouble. Sovereign citizens act in ways that are outside the traditional courtroom norms. They make statements that appear bizarre and nonsensical. They commonly read from internet scripts that supposedly teach them ways to win in the courtroom. To the unfamiliar courtroom official, their behavior may come across as that of someone who is lost and in need of guidance. In response, some judges attempt to work with the sovereign citizen to correct their thinking. However, the judge fails to recognize that the behavior of the sovereign citizen is deliberate, well thought out and often scripted. It is not a lack of understanding of American laws. It is instead a total rejection, by the sovereign citizen, of the legitimacy of the American government and the American judicial system. Sovereign citizens do not need education in the law or in courtroom procedure. They have rejected all U.S. laws. They have determined that the U.S. judicial system is without merit and is a farce in its entirety. They are not lost or in need of direction from the judge.

The sovereign citizen rejects the judicial system and has predetermined it to have no jurisdiction over them. By being patient and mistaking the intentions of the sovereign citizen, the judge unintentionally emboldens them. It appears to the sovereign citizen that their worthless arguments and maneuvers in the courtroom, have merit since the judge is so patiently entertaining the sovereign's maneuvers and verbal arguments. The patience of the judge only reinforces the misbehavior of the sovereign citizen. It also wastes time and court resources.

Many mistake the aberrant behavior of the sovereign citizen as being indicative of mental illness. Initially, it was not uncommon for judges to send sovereign citizens to be evaluated for mental illness. Court-mandated psychiatric evaluations, are far less common today. Studies consistently show that the vast majority of sovereign citizens are not mentally ill and are able to participate in the proceedings of their trials.

To remedy the problem of the sovereign citizen in the courtroom, all court personnel should be trained to recognize and identify sovereign citizen tactics and behavior. Training would enable the quick recognition of a sovereign citizen defendant. Once a sovereign citizen defendant has been identified, much time could be saved. The sovereign citizen is no more likely to be mentally ill than the non-sovereign citizen. The strange behavior of the sovereign citizen, the repeated claims that they "do not understand," is not a result of legitimate confusion but is a scripted response. These scripts to instruct the sovereign citizen on their behavior with the police or in the courtroom, can be readily purchased on the internet at prices ranging from $30–$300. If a sovereign citizen acts inappropriately in court, they should be held in contempt of court. Tolerating disruptive behavior only emboldens the sovereign citizen and all others attempting to utilize similar tactics in court.

An important goal of the judicial system should be to prevent the fraudulent filings of sovereign citizens from entering the courtroom. The Court of Queen's Bench of Alberta, the Superior Court in Canada, is much closer to achieving this goal. They have had considerable success with the implementation of a Master Order which requires the clerk to review any documents by a suspected problematic litigant for common signs of pseudolegal pleadings. Clerks are instructed to refuse any suspected fraudulent documents which are then returned to the filer who has an opportunity to correct the errors. The Master Order has been in place for four years. Impressively, most rejected applicants have never attempted to refile (McRoberts 2019). McRoberts (2019) believes that while clerks in American courts are prohibited from refusing filings, reform is possible within the current set of rules.

7.4 The Fight Against Domestic Terrorism

Bjelopera (2017) identified a fundamental problem at the federal level regarding the fight against domestic terrorism more broadly. He observes that there exists a clearly articulated regimen for identifying foreign terrorist organizations (FTO) but there is no comparable process in place for publicly identifying domestic terrorist organizations (Bjelopera 2017). Despite that being the case, the Department of Justice (DOJ) and FBI does publicly name domestic terrorist threats (Bjelopera 2017). As it stands, the FBI has identified sovereign citizens as being a domestic terrorist threat (Federal Bureau of Investigation 2011). Official labeling, of the sovereign citizen, as a domestic terrorist "organization," as opposed to terrorist "threat," could enhance the federal efforts to combat the sovereign citizen movement and potentially offer state and local agencies additional mechanisms for prosecution.

Relative to other domestic terrorist threats, too little scholarship has been devoted to sovereign citizens. Studies have been published but they are very few in number. There currently exists no mechanism for tracking nationwide statistics or incidents committed by sovereign citizens. Because of this, our government is limited in its ability to fully understand and combat the nature of the sovereign citizen threat. Given their beliefs about the illegitimacy of the U.S. government, sovereign citizens can be likened to anarchists. Their rejection of U.S. laws and their willingness to utilize violence in furtherance of their illegal behavior, makes them a dangerous threat to every law-abiding citizen in this country. Their illegal, criminal behavior serves no purpose other than furthering their own self-interests. More research is needed to understand the circumstances which lead to the adoption of sovereign citizen ideology

Sovereign citizens are a much greater threat than is recognized by the average American citizen. Many American citizens are completely unaware of the existence of sovereign citizens. Many have simply never heard the term "sovereign citizen." Sovereign citizen ideology is much more than a difference of opinion, that underlies behavior. Sovereign citizen ideology and behavior are antigovernment. Sovereign citizens are both terrorists and anarchists. Their behavior is that of outlaws. They would not describe themselves as being outlaws. After all, if all American laws are illegitimate, and the entire U.S. government, itself, is illegitimate, then there are no legitimate laws to be outside of.

There was a time, in the geographical area whose boundaries are currently those of the U.S., when the U.S. did not exist. Peoples living in the Americas, lived under the rules and laws of the British Empire. After a brutally fought war, after common displays of incredible bravery and with the undoubted help of divine providence, independence from Britain was obtained. There was no government, there were no rules. George Washington's military, proposed that he become the king of America. He quickly declined the offer. The wisdom of the day proposed a new type of government, the best that the mind of man could conceive. The tyrannies of other forms of government were understood, by our founding fathers. Every attempt was made to build a never-before-seen form of government. The American Constitution was the formula to create that new government. Everything that was to come, in the following decades and centuries, would follow the precise formula specified in the U.S. Constitution. The founding fathers tried to anticipate all the problems and complications that might arise. They specified how laws would be written and the branch of government that would write those laws. They did not assume that the branch that wrote the laws would be sufficient to judge the validity of the laws or the law's adherence to the Constitution. Congress wrote the laws, the judicial branch of government would determine their

7.4 The Fight Against Domestic Terrorism

validity. Thus, a law that Congress passed unanimously, could be overturned by the judicial branch of government. It is not enough that Congress pass a good and moral law. It must be a law that is allowed for by the American Constitution.

Not constitutional? Then, not a law. Any plaintiff could challenge the constitutionality of a law. However, it was possible that a judge could rule the law constitutional and thus rule against the plaintiff. The plaintiff need not be satisfied by the judge's verdict and could appeal the judge's verdict to a higher court. This appeal process could go on from appellate court to higher appellate court and then finally to the Supreme Court. The ruling of the Supreme Court, is the final word. No disagreement beyond that point is possible. That is how the founding fathers created the structure of this country. No sovereign citizen or citizen of any kind was to determine the validity of a law or more importantly, the interpretation of a law, or the Constitution.

The law was not up to self-interpretation. A law, every law, could only be interpreted by a judge and then a higher judge and perhaps a higher judge. Ultimately, only the Supreme Court justices would determine the validity and applicability of any and every law.

No citizen, sovereign or otherwise, can determine the validity of a law or interpret the American Constitution. This can only be done by the Supreme Court justices. Like it or not, love it or leave it, that is the structure of the country you live in. The Constitution does not allow for anything else. The law must be followed and anyone who does not follow the law, is and should be punished. Sovereign citizens and others like them with similar ideologies are an open threat to the U.S. The American government recognizes them as such, labeling them "domestic terrorists." Sovereign citizens exist in small towns, large cities and in the far wilderness of Alaska.

Sovereign citizens have killed ordinary American citizens but are better known for their murder of police officers. Sovereign citizens must be punished to the full extent of the law. Their crimes, infractions and misdemeanors, must not be overlooked or plea bargained. They are not, unintelligent, ill-informed, individuals, deserving of our indulgence. They are terrorists. They live outside the law. They believe the American government does not exist. They believe that no U.S. law is applicable to them, that no court in the U.S. has power over them. They believe that they may move into any vacant home. They believe, when they are stopped or arrested by police officers, that they have the right to kill them.

The sanctity of a government is guaranteed by its laws. Sovereign citizens have a right to their opinion but not the right to live outside the law. They must be more commonly recognized for the threat that they currently pose and also for the future threat posed, as this antigovernment movement grows.

Sovereign citizens do run for political office. They currently sit on juries. Their numbers are small but they are growing. They can be found in every state of our union. Their growth poses the same existential threat to our country, as cancer cells do to our bodies.

References

Beirich, H. (Fall, 2012). Two North Carolina detectives build program for dealing with 'soveriegn citizens.' *Southern Povery Law Center*. Retireved from https://www.splcenter.org/fighting-hate/intelligence-report/2012/two-north-carolina-detectives-build-program-dealing-sovereign-citizens

Bjelopera, J. P. (2017). Domestic terrorism: An overview. Congressional Research Service. Retrieved from https://fas.org/sgp/crs/terror/R44921.pdf

Federal Bureau of Investigation. (2011). Sovereign Citizens: A Growing Domestic Threat to Law Enforcement. Washington, DC: Federal Bureau of Investigation, Counterterrorism Division. Retrieved from https://leb.fbi.gov/articles/featured-articles/sovereign-citizens-a-growing-domestic-threat-to-law-enforcement.

Givens, L., & King, M. (2019, September 12). Realtor says squatting is becoming a greater problem across Georgia. *11Alive*. Retrieved from https://www.11alive.com/article/news/local/realtor-says-squatting-becoming-greater-problem/85-3f4740d1-5057-4988-90c9-99ef9ebdef0b

Hate Crimes & The Threat of Domestic Terrorism. (2012). Hearing before the Subcommittee on the Constitution, Civil Rights and Human Rights of the Committee on the Judiciary United States Senate. 112th Cong. (testimony of Daryl Johnson).

House Bill N0.1769. (2018). 99th General assembly. *Senate Committee Substitute* (Missouri).

Lakin, M. (2017, March 19). Records: Bogus liens by East Tennessee 'Sovereign citizens' topped $2B. *Knoxville News Sentinel*. Retrieved from https://www.knoxnews.com/story/news/crime/2017/03/19/records-bogus-liens-sovereigns-topped-2-billion/99257156/

Lockhead, C. (2019, May 2). Nevada officials work to fight sovereign citizens movement. *Las Vegas Review-Journal*. Retrieved from https://www.reviewjournal.com/news/politics-and-government/2019-legislature/nevada-officials-work-to-fight-sovereign-citizens-movement-1654960/

March-Safbom, T. (2018). Weapons of mass distraction: Strategies for countering the paper terrorism of sovereign citizens. *Homeland Security Affairs*. Retrieved from https://www.hsaj.org/articles/14539

McRoberts, C. (2019). Tinfoil hats and powdered wigs: Thoughts on pseudolaw. *Washburn Law Journal, 58*, 637–668. Retrieved from https://contentdm.washburnlaw.edu/digital/collection/wlj/id/7122/

Parker, G. F. (2014). Competence to stand trial evaluations of sovereign citizens: A case series and primer of odd political and legal beliefs. *The Journal of the American Academy of Psychiatry and the Law, 42*(3), 338–349. Retrieved from http://jaapl.org/content/42/3/338.

Smith, T. (2019, September 23). What you don't know about sovereign citizens can hurt you. *In Homeland Security*. Retrieved from https://inhomelandsecurity.com/what-you-dont-know-about-sovereign-citizens-can-hurt-you/

Stockler, A. (2019, September 14). Florida man gets 40 years for creating fake international court, intimidating government officials. *Newsweek*. Retrieved from https://www.newsweek.com/randal-rosado-florida-man-international-court-sovereign-citizen-1459274

Weir, J. P. (2015). Sovereign citizens: A reasoned response to the madness. *Lewis & Clark Law Review, 19(3)*, 829–870. Retrieved from https://law.lclark.edu/live/files/20846-lcb193art12weirpdf.

Whitmire, L. (2015, April 22). Sovereign citizen movement: Is it dangerous? *Mansfield News Journal*. Retrieved from https://www.mansfieldnewsjournal.com/story/news/local/2015/04/22/sovereign-citizens-followup/26201909/.

Correction to: Sovereign Citizens: A Psychological and Criminological Analysis

Correction to:
C. M. Sarteschi, *Sovereign Citizens*, SpringerBriefs in Psychology, https://doi.org/10.1007/978-3-030-45851-5

"Owing to an error on the part of the publisher, the first paragraphs of the chapters were omitted in the chapter PDF files and in print in the initially published version of this book. They were instead included in the online abstracts. This has now been corrected, and the paragraphs have been added to the chapter opening pages. This correction has caused a repagination of the book."

The updated online versions of these chapters can be found at
https://doi.org/10.1007/978-3-030-45851-5_1
https://doi.org/10.1007/978-3-030-45851-5_2
https://doi.org/10.1007/978-3-030-45851-5_3
https://doi.org/10.1007/978-3-030-45851-5_5
https://doi.org/10.1007/978-3-030-45851-5_6
https://doi.org/10.1007/978-3-030-45851-5

© The Author(s), under exclusive license to Springer Nature Switzerland AG 2020
C. M. Sarteschi, *Sovereign Citizens*, SpringerBriefs in Psychology,
https://doi.org/10.1007/978-3-030-45851-5_8

GPSR Compliance
The European Union's (EU) General Product Safety Regulation (GPSR) is a set
of rules that requires consumer products to be safe and our obligations to
ensure this.

If you have any concerns about our products, you can contact us on

ProductSafety@springernature.com

In case Publisher is established outside the EU, the EU authorized
representative is:

Springer Nature Customer Service Center GmbH
Europaplatz 3
69115 Heidelberg, Germany